papercrafting

In No Time

50 inspirational projects crafted from paper

CLARE YOUNGS

CICO BOOKS

LONDON NEW YORK

Published in 2010 by CICO Books
An imprint of Ryland Peters & Small Ltd
20–21 Jockey's Fields   519 Broadway, 5th Floor
London WC1R 4BW   New York, NY 10012

www.cicobooks.com

10 9 8 7 6 5 4 3 2

A CIP catalog record for this book is available from
the Library of Congress and the British Library.

ISBN: 978 1 907030 81 9

Printed in China

Editor: Marie Clayton
Design: Jacqui Caulton
Style photography: Claire Richardson
Step photography: Martin Norris

For digital editions, visit
www.cicobooks.com/apps.php

Contents

Introduction

Paper is the perfect craft material: cheap, readily available, and endlessly versatile. Craftsmen have explored the possibilities of creating beautiful paper pieces for centuries—by cutting, folding, tearing, curling, or gluing, a simple sheet of paper can be transformed into a stunning artwork, a thoughtful gift, or an original greetings card. You don't need an expensive array of tools and materials, while the techniques of the craft are easy and fun! There is something for everyone in this book and I have taken inspiration from around the world: the traditional art of paper cutting in Poland; the decorative arts of Mexico; the craft of paperfolding from Japan. With today's hectic lifestyles, not everyone has time to devote to a craft, so I have created a variety of projects, some of which take only minutes. Chapter One has wonderful pieces for the home, such as the colorful Oriental fan lampshade, while Chapter Two has items for kids—try the delightful sausage dog. In Chapter Three, there are great gifts and striking giftwrap; Chapter Four covers greetings cards; and Chapter Five has items for parties. Papercraft may be an ancient tradition, but the ideas here are fresh and contemporary, and in a world where technology and cyber entertainment are the norm, it is very satisfying to make something by hand. Have the confidence to experiment and develop your own ideas to reveal the artistic creativity that is within all of us.

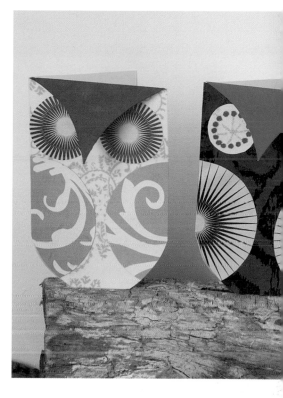

chapter one
Living spaces

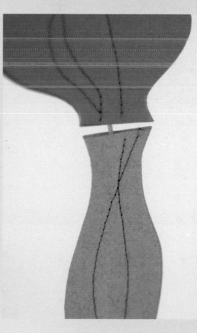

Framed bird paper cut

This is artwork on a big scale, ideal for framing. It is designed in the style of a Polish paper cut, but the bird is a popular motif frequently appearing in folk art around the world. Although making paper cuts like this is an old craft, the bright colors and stylishly bold graphic look work perfectly in a modern interior.

you will need:

Bird, flower and leaf templates on page 159

Tracing paper

Pencil

14 x 18in. (35 x 45cm) sheet of thin white paper

Scalpel or craft knife

Cutting mat

Metal ruler

Small piece of orange paper

1½ x 20in. (4 x 50cm) length of green paper

14 x 18in. (35 x 45cm) sheet of pink paper

Glue stick

16 x 20in. (40 x 50cm) sheet of thick white paper

Picture frame

1 Trace the bird template and transfer it onto some thin white paper. Use a scalpel or craft knife to cut out the design carefully.

2 Trace the templates to transfer the flower and leaf vein to the orange paper, and the leaf to the green paper. Cut out the shapes.

3 Take the large sheet of pink paper and tear off a strip approx. 2in. (5cm) wide down the left side to make an uneven textured edge.

4 Stick the sheet of pink paper onto the right-hand side of the sheet of thick white paper, approx. 1in. (2.5cm) in from the top, bottom, and the right-hand end. Cut a strip of green paper approx. 1¾ x 14in. (4 x 35cm) and stick it down approx. 1in. (2.5cm) in from the left-hand edge of the white paper and aligned with the top and bottom edge of the pink sheet.

5 Stick the orange leaf vein to the back of the leaf so that it shows through the slit. Stick the bird, flower, and leaf in position, then frame the finished artwork.

Origami fan lampshade

This is such a simple way to jazz up a plain lampshade. You can buy packs of Japanese origami papers in craft stores designs are gorgeous and you can use every one of them in this project! I found this little Oriental-inspired lamp stand at a flea market but the shade would look just as good on a plain stand.

you will need:

Pack of 6in. (15cm) squares of Japanese origami paper

Scissors

Ruler

Glue stick

Plain lampshade

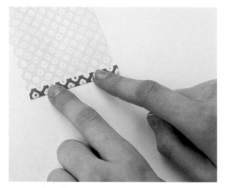

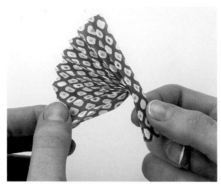

1 Cut each square in half. Lay one oblong on a flat surface pattern side down. Fold over a strip approx. ¼in. (6mm) wide along one short end.

2 Turn the paper over and fold back a strip to match the first fold, to create a zigzag. Carry on folding backward and forward until you get to the end. Make a fold 1in. (2.5cm) up from the base. Pinching the bottom section between your fingers, fold it over to the side while fanning out the top section.

3 Cut off approx ⅜in. (1cm) from the bottom section. The fan is now ready to be stuck down on the shade. Make a whole pile of fans in assorted colors and patterns—if you have any leftover fans, you can use them on greetings cards or giftwrap.

4 Place a blob of glue at the base of the fan and stick it to the top of the lampshade. Stick the fans all around the top of the shade in a row, overlapping the previous one each time.

5 Carry on down the shade row by row, overlapping the fans to fill any gaps, until you are nearly at the base. For the last row, stick the fans upside down, tucking the base behind the spread-out fans of the previous row.

Wreath

Shades of blue, green, and gold give a touch of elegance to this pretty wreath, used here as a wall decoration. It is made by sticking individual leaves onto a cardstock circle, so you can make it in any size by adjusting the size of the backing. Use reds, greens, and gold for a beautiful Christmas wreath.

1 Find something large to draw around as a guide for your outer circle—I used a round tray. Use something smaller such as a plate to draw the inner circle, placing it by eye in the center of the sheet of foamboard.

2 Use a scalpel or craft knife to cut out the circular shape and the central hole.

3 Trace the template and use it to mark out the leaf shapes on a selection of patterned and colored paper. You can vary the width of the leaves, as long as the lengths are similar. You could also cut by eye to speed up the process.

4 Score down the center of each leaf from tip to base, varying the curve as you go. Use the tip of the knife to just mark the surface of the paper, making sure you do not cut right through. Crease along the scored line of each leaf to make the 3D-shaped leaves.

5 Flatten the end of a leaf and place a dab of glue on the underside. Position it on the base and hold it in place while it dries for a short time, before moving on to the next one. Position the leaves alongside each other across the width of the wreath.

6 Start another row, tucking the ends out of sight under the first row of leaves. Don't worry about getting the spaces even—just carry on sticking the leaves around until you have covered the entire circle.

Lollipop flowers

Place these jolly flowers and leaves in a row along a mantel shelf or pop a whole bunch into a pretty vase for a touch of spring cheer all the year round. I found these thin wooden sticks for the stems in a craft store but you could use garden sticks painted white, or round Popsicle (lolly) sticks.

you will need:

Flower and leaf templates on page 160

Tracing paper

Pencil

Sheets of paper in contrasting colors

Scissors

Scalpel or craft knife

Cutting mat

Pieces of thin cardstock

Narrow stick for stem of each flower

Glue stick

1 These flowers have two, three, or four layers; the directions are for the spiky flower with three layers. Trace the templates and transfer the flower and leaf shapes onto colored paper.

2 Cut out the flower and leaf shapes. Cut out the pattern on the flower. Trace and cut the same outlines from thin cardstock to make the backing for the flower and leaf shapes.

3 Lay the stick along the center of the cardstock backing flower and place the leaf shape further down the stick.

4 Stick the next layer of the flower and the leaf section on top, sandwiching the stick between them. Trace and cut the top layer of the flower from contrasting colored paper.

5 Stick the top layer of the flower in position, placing it to one side. Keep adding layers in the same way for flowers with more layers. If displaying several flowers, cut the stems to various lengths.

Sunflower

I like making things out of paper purely for decorative reasons, and this sunflower is one of those projects. Whether you hang it on a wall, place it on a mantelpiece, or use it as a centerpiece for a dinner party, it will always be a talking point. I used the covers of vintage music scores because I love the aged color of the paper and the beautiful script lettering of days gone by.

you will need:

Sheet of thin white tabloid size (A3) cardstock

Ruler

Scalpel or craft knife

Cutting mat

Scissors

Glue stick

Vintage sheet music

Sunflower petal template on page 161

Tracing paper

Pencil

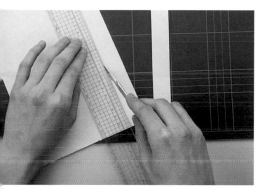

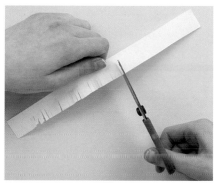

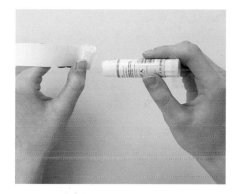

1 Measure and then cut some strips of thin white cardstock, each 1in. (2.5cm) wide.

2 Snip a fringe all along one long side, cutting down approx. ⅝in. (15mm) and making the snips approx. ¹⁄₁₆in. (2mm) apart.

3 Take the first strip and start coiling it up, placing a dab of glue along the unfringed edge every so often to hold the coil in place as you go. When you have finished winding one piece, take another and secure the end with glue. Carry on winding in the same way.

4 Continue until you have a disk approx. 3¼in. (8cm) across. Cut some strips ⅞in. (2cm) wide and 2in. (5cm) long from plain sections of the sheet music. Fold in half and stick the ends together, then stick the glued ends to the underside of the disk to create the first circle of petals.

  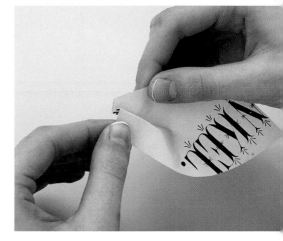

5 Trace over the sunflower petal template and use it to draw a selection of petals on interesting areas of the sheet music.

6 Cut out the petals using the scissors. Vary the width if you like— you do not have to fuss about getting them all the same size.

7 Make a small fold in the straight base to give each petal a gently curving shape.

8 Stick these petals in position behind the first circle of petals, overlapping them all the way around the center of the flower.

Paper know-how

When working with vintage paper, it is important to find good-quality sheets that still have an inherent strength. Some types of antique paper are quite soft and delicate, so are not only hard to work with but may also cause your project to disintegrate quickly.

Hanging cutout birds

Based on classic folk art motifs, the vibrant splashes of color on these birds catch the eye and add interest, so the brighter the backing paper the better! Hang them on sticks, or use to make a baby's mobile.

you will need:

Bird template on page 161

Tracing paper

Pencil

Sheet of white cardstock

Scalpel or craft knife

Cutting board

Scissors or a bone folder for scoring

Paper twine

Ruler

Masking tape

Scrap of patterned paper

Glue stick

¼in. (6mm) hole punch

Hammer

1 Trace one of the bird templates and transfer it to the white cardstock. Cut out two identical bird shapes, one for the front and one for the back, with a scalpel or craft knife.

2 Trace the shapes for the cutout pattern and transfer onto the front section of the bird. Cut the side lines using a scalpel or craft knife, making sure you do not cut the base line because this will be scored.

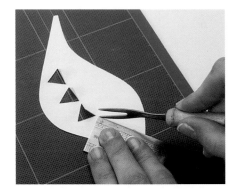

3 Score the base line on each of the cutout shapes and bend back the cutout sections.

4 Cut a piece of twine about 8in. (20cm) long and fold in half. Place it vertically down the center of the back section of the bird, with the looped end sticking out about 2¼in. (5.5cm). Secure the twine with a small piece of masking tape.

5 Place a piece of patterned paper over the back of the cutouts on the front section of the bird, with the pattern facing the bird. Secure with a few dabs of glue.

6 Glue the back and front sections of the bird together, with wrong sides facing. To finish, punch a hole for the eye with the hammer and hole punch.

Paper cut woodland scene

This woodland scene with the cheeky fox in the foreground has a charming folk art quality. You can make it to fit whatever size of square frame you choose.

you will need:

Tree template on page 162

Tracing paper

Pencil

Sheet of white letter size (A4) paper

Cutting mat

Scalpel or craft knife

Fox template on page 162

Small piece of drawing (cartridge) paper

Square picture frame

Contrasting color letter size (A4) paper

Glue stick

1 Trace the template of the tree and transfer it to a piece of white paper. Cut the paper to the size of the picture frame, centering the tree in the square.

2 Place the paper onto a cutting mat and start cutting out the shapes with a sharp scalpel or craft knife.

3 Trace the template of the front fox piece and transfer it onto the drawing (cartridge) paper. Cut out the fox section. Score the flaps and bend them back.

4 Remove the glass from the frame and place the contrast color paper into the back. Place the tree cutout in position on top and hold in place with a couple of dabs of glue.

5 Add dabs of glue to the flaps on the front fox piece and stick in position on one side edge and the bottom of the frame.

Stitched retro mobile

Mobiles make an interesting alternative to flat artwork and they do not have to be for children—grownups enjoy them too! They make an unusual focal point in a room, catching the eye as they twist and turn.

you will need:

Retro template on page 162

Tracing paper

Pencil

Sheets of colored letter size (A4) paper

Scissors

String

Masking tape or clear adhesive tape

Soft pencil

Sewing machine and thread

Soft eraser

1 Trace the templates and transfer the shapes onto colored paper.

2 Cut out the shapes with scissors. You need two cutouts in each color and shape.

3 Lay one set of pieces down in a row on a flat surface. Place a length of string down the center of the shapes and secure with a piece of tape on each shape. Make sure you leave some extra string at the top to hang the mobile.

4 Place the matching piece over the first shape and, with a soft pencil, draw some wavy lines going from the top of the shape down to the bottom. Vary the curve of the lines and overlap them sometimes. Repeat with the other shapes.

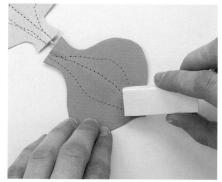

5 Sew the lines with a sewing machine to join the two sets of pieces together along the length of the string. Use a soft eraser to rub out any pencil lines that show. Make more mobile strings in the same way.

Mobile without stitching

If you do not want to use a sewing machine, you could just glue the two sides together, but the stitching does add a much more interesting design element.

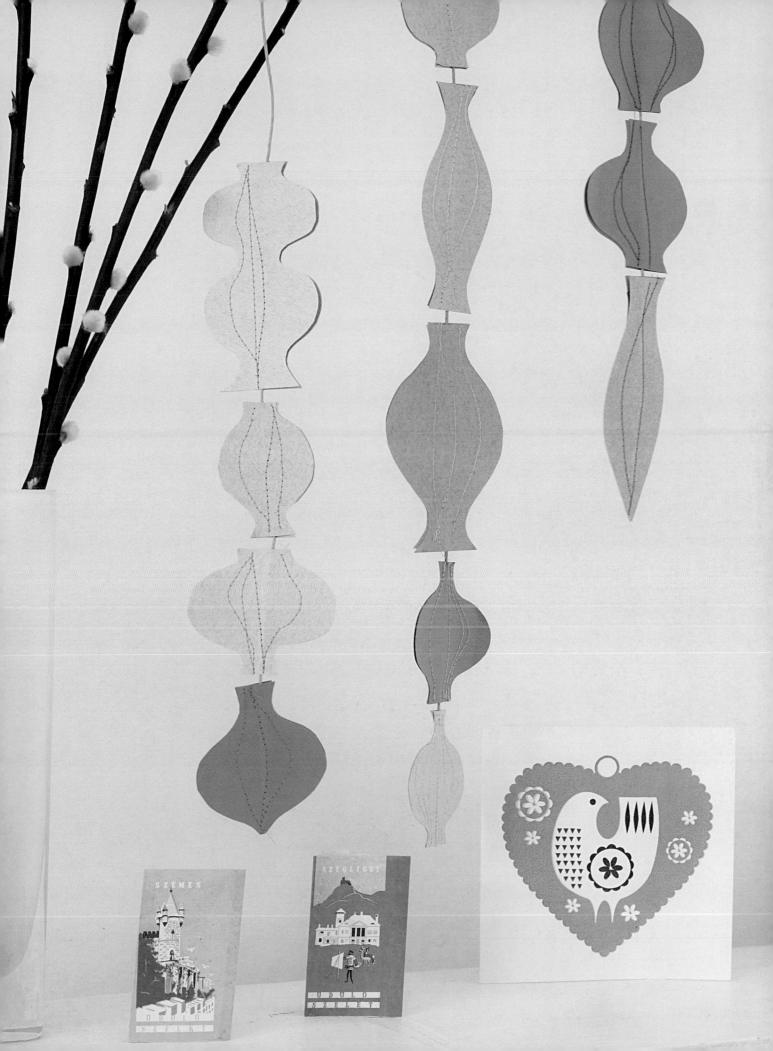

Recycled paper bowls

I love working with paper; you can take something as ordinary as a few pages torn from a magazine and create a unique and beautiful object. You can use any scrap paper for these little bowls—I wanted to experiment with color, so I folded together solid color and strips of music score paper. Make a few in different sizes, display them inside each other, and they become almost sculptural.

you will need:

Sheets of music score paper
Ruler
Pencil
Scalpel or craft knife
Cutting mat
Glue stick
Sheets of colored paper

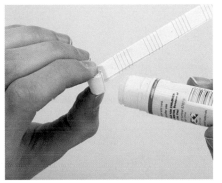

1 For the base I used the music score paper on its own, adding color only on the sides. Cut strips down the length of the paper measuring ⅞in. (2cm) in width. Fold the strips in half and half again.

2 Start winding one of the folded strips tightly to make a flat coil, adding some dabs of glue to secure as you go. When you have finished one strip, carry on with the next, adding a dab of glue to fasten the ends.

3 When the base has reached the desired width, begin adding some color. Cut a strip of music score paper ⅞in. (2cm) wide and one strip of brightly colored paper the same width. Slot them together so that you have a strip with one side music score and the other side colored.

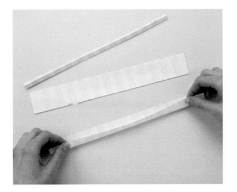

5 Carry on going, adding dabs of glue at intervals to secure the strips until the sides of the bowl have reached the desired height. Add a final dab of glue to secure the ends.

4 Start winding around the base with the music score side on the inside. As you wind, place the new strip about halfway up the last strip, so that you begin to build up the sides of the bowl.

Paper chandelier

Create a stunning focal point for your lounge or dining room with this beautiful chandelier, which will be much admired by your friends. This style of chandelier originates from Poland, a country with a history of paper craftsmanship, and they are usually made from brightly colored paper and tissue. I wanted to make this one in shades of white and cream, so I have used pages from old books to make the flower shapes.

you will need:

Circle template on page 163

Tracing paper

Pencil

Crepe paper

Scissors

Glue stick

Flower templates on page 163

Pages from an old book or a magazine

Sheets of cream paper

Small piece of corrugated cardstock

Large needle

Thin string

Metal ruler

Scalpel or craft knife

Cutting mat

Thick brown cardstock, flexible enough to bend into a circle

Double-sided tape

Quick-drying strong glue

1 Trace the template and use it to cut out lots of circles from the crepe paper. The easiest way is to hold the template up against folded crepe paper so that you can cut several circles at once. Don't worry about perfect circles.

2 Place a dab of glue in the center of a circle and stick the next circle on top. Repeat with another six circles.

3 When the glue has dried, pinch together the base of the circles in the middle and scrunch them up to form a flower. You will need 14 crepe flowers in total.

4 Use the flower templates to cut out the three different size flower shapes using the same method as for the crepe paper circles. Cut half from white paper from an old book and half in a cream color for contrast. You will need 147 small flowers, 21 medium flowers, and 16 large flowers.

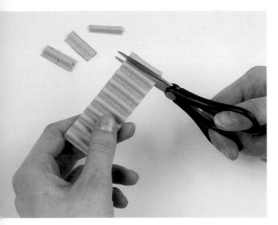

5 Cut a piece of corrugated cardstock into 1¼in. (3cm) wide strips and then cut in between each tube section to create 196 little tubes.

6 Thread a large needle with thin string, tie a knot at the end, and thread one of the crepe paper flowers onto the string, placing the needle through the front middle of the flower.

7 Thread one of the large flower shapes onto the string, followed by a corrugated tube, then another large flower shape. Alternating white and cream flowers, continue threading with three medium flowers and then five small ones, with a tube between each flower. Finish with a tube. Tie a knot at the end. Repeat to make seven flower-end strings in total. Follow this method to make 14 strings of eight small flowers, each starting and ending with a tube.

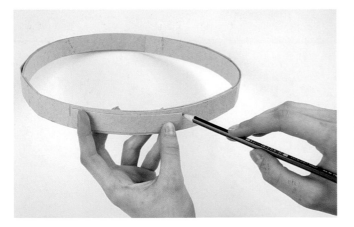

8 Cut three strips of thick cardstock, each ⅞in. (2cm) wide and approx. 36in. (90cm) in length. Curve one strip around into a hoop, overlap by about 4in. (10cm), and secure with some double-sided tape. Place double-sided tape along the other two strips of cardstock, and then remove the backing and wrap one of the strips around the hoop, cutting off any overlap. Repeat with the third strip of cardstock to make a hoop of three layers. Divide the hoop into seven equal sections and mark with a pencil on the inside.

9 Place a piece of double-sided tape at each mark. Peel back the tape backing on the first two sections. Take one of the seven flower-end strings and press the string at the tube end firmly onto the double-sided tape. Stick the end of one of the 14 small flower strings next to this and loop the other end around to the next piece of double-sided tape.

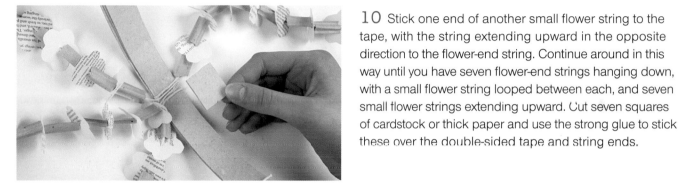

10 Stick one end of another small flower string to the tape, with the string extending upward in the opposite direction to the flower-end string. Continue around in this way until you have seven flower-end strings hanging down, with a small flower string looped between each, and seven small flower strings extending upward. Cut seven squares of cardstock or thick paper and use the strong glue to stick these over the double-sided tape and string ends.

11 Stick the last two large flowers together, sandwiching all the ends of the strings at the top of the chandelier in between them.

12 Use a quick-drying strong glue to stick the remaining seven crepe flowers on the outside of the hoop at each of the seven sections.

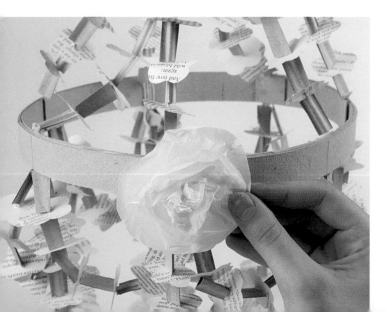

Tealight houses

This is one of my favorite projects, with a simple but stylish Scandinavian look that is very appealing. Set the finished row of houses up on the mantelshelf with a tealight behind each house section—the open windows and doors will be lit with a warm glow, making a charming display.

you will need:

Houses template on page 163
Tracing paper
Pencil
9 x 20in. (22 x 50cm) thin white cardstock
Metal ruler
Scalpel or craft knife
Cutting mat
Tealights

1 Trace the houses template and carefully transfer the outline onto the thin white cardstock.

2 Using a scalpel or craft knife, cut out the outline of the houses. Cut out the windows and decorations on the houses, taking care not to cut the indicated score lines.

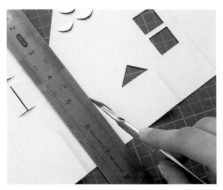

3 Score the fold lines where indicated and fold back. Score down between each house.

4 Fold one house forward and one house back to make a corrugated row of houses. Place a tealight behind each house at a safe distance.

Love tealight lanterns

Create a romantic atmosphere with these delightful paper lanterns. Made from brown paper and colored tissue, they create a warm, welcoming glow and would make a stylish centerpiece for the dining table.

you will need:

4 large glass tealight holders or heatproof glass tumblers

Metal ruler	Tracing paper
Pencil	⅜in. (4mm) hole punch
Sheets of brown paper	Hammer
Scalpel or craft knife	Sheets of colored tissue
Cutting mat	Glue stick
Letter templates on page 163	Tealights

1 Measure one of the tealight holders or heatproof glass tumblers and cut a piece of brown paper the same height and long enough to go around the outside with a ¼in. (6mm) overlap. Trace the design for the cutout letter and transfer it to the center of the brown paper.

2 Use a scalpel or craft knife and the hole punch and hammer to cut out the design carefully.

4 Curve the brown paper into a cylinder and glue down the overlap edge to form a tube. Slip the tube over the tealight holder or glass tumbler, then place a tealight inside.

3 Cut a square of colored tissue paper large enough to cover the cutout design. Glue it over the area of the design on the reverse.

chapter two
For kids

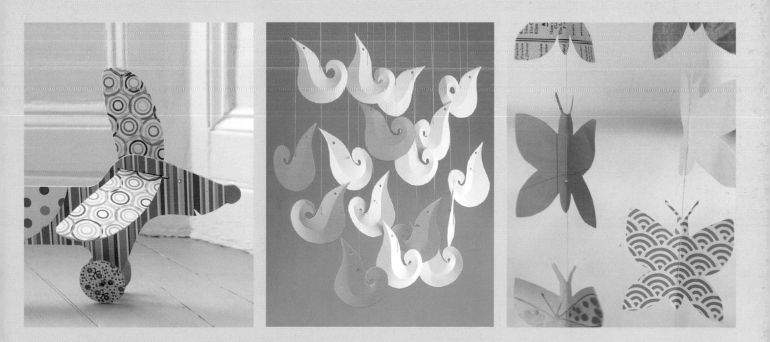

Bird boxes

The bright colors used for this bird and bird box really catch the eye, while the simple shapes mean it is very easy to make. A row of these boxes arranged on a shelf or mantelpiece would create an attractive feature—or hang up one or more to add interest to a dull corner.

you will need:

Bird box template on page 164

Pencil

Metal ruler

12 x 22in. (30 x 55cm) thin white cardstock

Scalpel or craft knife

Cutting mat

Sheets of patterned paper in at least three different designs

Glue stick

Reel of thread or compass

³⁄₁₆in. (4mm) hole punch

Hammer

Bone folder

Bird template on page 164

Tracing paper

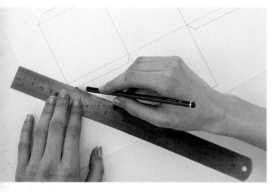

1 Draw up the shape of the bird box onto the thin white cardstock by following the template on page 164.

2 Cut around the outer outline of the bird box carefully, using a scalpel or craft knife and a metal ruler.

3 Using the same measurements as for the cardstock base, cut out different pieces of patterned paper and glue them on to cover the front and sides of the bird box.

4 Draw around a large reel of thread or use a compass to mark a circle about 1¼in. (3cm) in diameter on the front panel, with the top edge 1¾in. (4.5cm) down from the top of the panel. Cut out the circle with the craft knife or scalpel.

5 Using the hole punch and hammer, cut a small hole ⁷⁄₁₆in. (1cm) below the larger hole.

ENGLISH TRADITION IN DESIGN

BRITISH MOT...

EDIBLE FUNGI

UR : THE FIRST PHASES

WILD FLOWERS OF THE CHALK

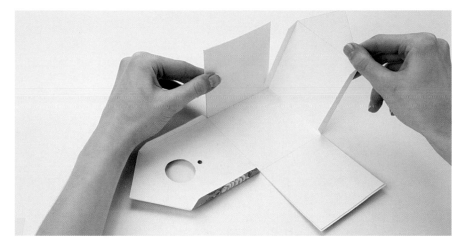

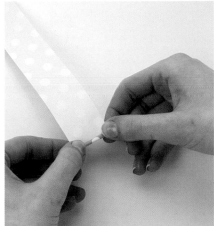

6 Score all the fold lines on the flaps and sides with the bone folder. Crease along the score lines to form the box shape. Place glue along the flaps and stick the shape together to form the box.

7 To make the perch, take a strip of offcut paper about 1¼in. (3cm) wide and roll it up tightly until it fits snugly inside the smaller hole of the bird box.

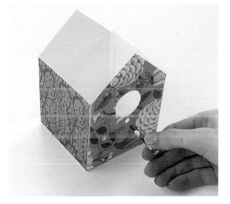

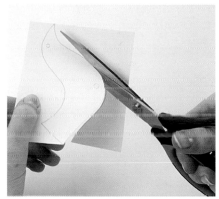

8 Cut off any excess paper and glue down the edge of the paper to secure. Place the perch in the small hole in the front panel.

9 Glue a piece of patterned paper to a piece of thin cardstock approx. 4½ x 2¾in. (11 x 7cm). Trace the bird shape from the template and transfer it to the card. Cut out the bird and then punch a hole ⅜in. (9mm) up from the center bottom edge. Punch another hole for the eye. Slide the bird onto the perch.

10 To make the roof, glue a piece of patterned paper to a piece of cardstock 5¾ x 4½in. (14.5 x 11.5cm). Lightly score a line with the bone folder across the width in the center of the roof section. Crease along the score line and bend into the roof shape. Place the roof on the bird box.

Curly tailed birds and nest

These curly tailed birds can be made into a mobile, or arranged to perch on a colorful nest. The nest variation would also be a great way to present tiny chocolate eggs on Easter morning!

you will need:

Bird template on page 164
Tracing paper
Pencil
Sheet of thick white letter size (A4) drawing (cartridge) paper
Scalpel or craft knife
Cutting mat
¼in. (6mm) hole punch
Hammer

Old maps (for the nest)
Needle and thick thread (for a mobile)

1 Trace the bird from the template and transfer the shape onto the white drawing (cartridge) paper.

2 Cut out the bird shape carefully with the scalpel or craft knife and use the hole punch and hammer to make the eye.

3 Use the scalpel to score the curved line down the center of the bird shape. The blade must just mark the surface of the paper, not go right through. Start at the beak and apply gentle pressure to draw the blade around the curve, ending at the center of the tail.

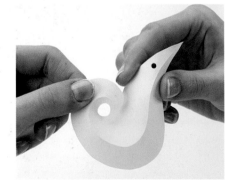

4 Gently squeeze the bird into shape. Pinch gently along the score line and push the tail end in toward the body of the bird in a circular movement. This does take a bit of practice!

5 For the nest, shred an old map into strips ⅛–14in. (3–5mm) wide. Bundle a few together to form a nest shape, using your hands to press in the middle of the nest, gathering any stray bits and winding them around the outer part of the nest.

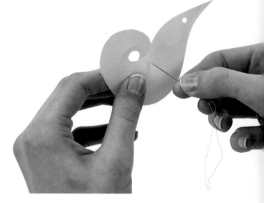

6 If you are making a mobile, stitch through the bird with the needle and thread, and secure with a knot.

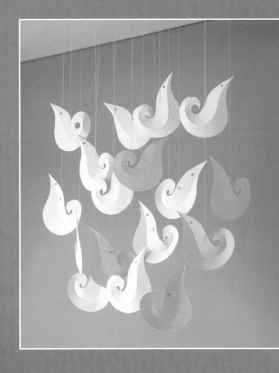

Steamboat

I have a large collection of paper, old labels, packaging, postcards, and giftwrap. In this project, such interesting scraps can be put to good use. If you have a child, paintings and drawings quickly mount up but there is only so much room on the wall, so why not use some of them to make colorful flags?

you will need:

Boat template on page 165

Tracing paper

Pencil

Metal ruler

Scalpel or craft knife

Cutting mat

16 x 24in. (40 x 60cm) sheet of thick cardstock or foamboard

Glue stick

Sheets of graph paper

Sheets of patterned paper

Old map or similar design in blue

String

Strong tape

1 Use the tracing paper to transfer the shape of the hull template onto the cardstock or foamboard. Cut out the hull shape.

2 Measure and cut out a mast ⅞in. (2cm) wide and 16in. (40cm) in length and stick it halfway along the boat. Cover both the hull and the mast with a background paper, such as graph paper.

3 Cut out pieces of paper to decorate the funnel and the bridge, and stick them down. Trace the waves from the template onto a blue area of the map or the blue design paper. Cut out and stick in position on the hull.

4 Cut out some large circles for the portholes and stick in position along the hull. Cut out a flag to use at the top of the masthead.

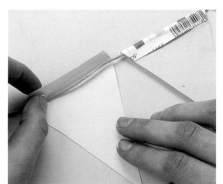

5 Cut two 22in. (56cm) pieces of string. Cut out ten flags from an assortment of patterned paper using the templates. Fold over the flaps at the top of each flag. Space the flags out evenly along each string. Stick in place by gluing the flap and folding it over the string.

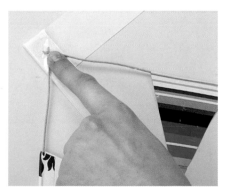

6 Secure the lengths of bunting with a piece of strong tape at the top of the mast and at the tips of the boat.

Butterfly room divider

This modern interpretation of the classic beaded curtain is an excellent opportunity to use up those attractive scraps of paper you have collected. The project is very simple and a great one to get the kids involved in. Try experimenting with other shapes, too, like a simple star and crescent moon combination for a bedroom.

you will need:

Scraps of patterned paper
Butterfly template on page 165
Tracing paper
Pencil
Scissors
Needle
Long strands of strong thread

1 Fold small scraps of paper in half. Trace the butterfly from the template and transfer onto the folded pieces of paper with the center of the butterfly aligned with the fold.

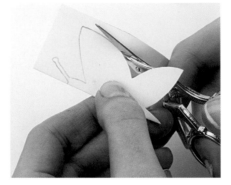

2 Cut out the butterfly shape from the folded paper using a small pair of scissors.

3 Cut out a selection of several different butterflies in a variety of colors and patterns.

4 Using a needle and strong thread, join the butterflies together by placing one long stitch along the center fold. Space the butterflies evenly along the thread and hang. Repeat to create as many hanging threads as you need.

Decorative wrap

Use a strand of butterflies to tie around a parcel. Even plain brown paper can be transformed into pretty and original giftwrap.

Sausage dog

You can make so many unusual things out of paper or card, even this cute pull-along sausage dog! He would look lovely sitting on a shelf in a child's bedroom. You could also make a few small puppies and display them all in a row. Use different prints for their jackets... adorable!

you will need:

Dog template on page 166

Tracing paper

Pencil

16½ x 12in. (42 x 30cm) sheet of thick cardstock or foamboard

Scalpel or craft knife

Cutting mat

Glue stick

Sheets of patterned paper

¼in. (6mm) hole punch

Hammer

³⁄₁₆in. (4mm) hole punch

Small piece of thin cardstock

2 small sheets plain colored paper

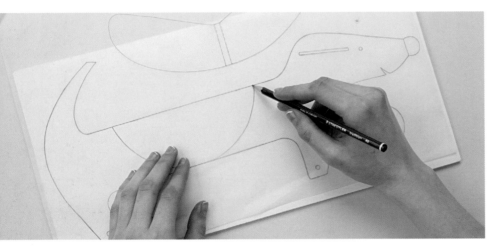

1 Trace the templates and transfer the shape for the body onto a piece of thick cardstock or foamboard. Cut out the body shape with a scalpel or craft knife.

2 Stick the cardstock body shape to the back of one of the sheets of patterned paper. Cut around the body with the scalpel or craft knife to trim off the excess paper.

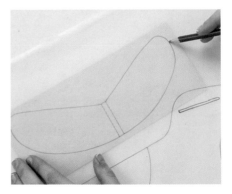

3 Turn the body over and repeat to cover the other side. Use the tracing you made in step 1 to transfer the mouth, eye, and slot for the ears.

4 Cut out the mouth and ear slot with the knife. Use the ¼in. (6mm) hole punch for the eye. Use the ³⁄₁₆in. (4mm) hole punch to make a hole at the bottom of each leg, centered approx ³⁄₈in. (1cm) up from the edge.

5 Use the tracing paper to transfer the shape for the ears onto some thin cardstock. Cut out.

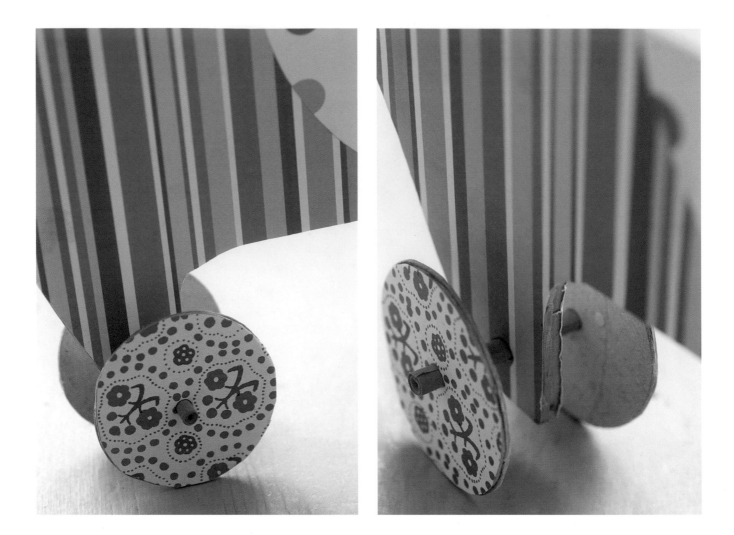

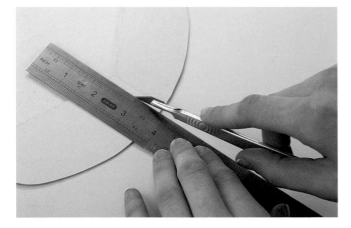

6 Cover the ears with some contrasting patterned paper on both sides in the same way as you did for the body. Score the lines where indicated and bend the cardstock to make two floppy ears.

7 To make the axle for the wheels, cut out a piece of paper approx. 2in. (5cm) in width and 2½in. (6.5cm) in length and roll up tightly to form a tube. Before adding a dab of glue to stop it unrolling, check it fits snugly in the hole. You may have to cut a little bit from the length to make the axle smaller in diameter. Repeat to make a second axle.

  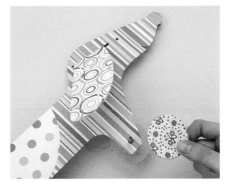

8 Use the template as a guide to cut out four wheels from the thick cardstock or foamboard. Cover both sides in patterned paper in the same way you covered the body. Use the ³⁄₁₆in. (4mm) hole punch to make a hole in the center of each wheel.

9 Use the template to transfer the semicircles for the coat to a contrasting sheet of patterned paper. Cut out the semicircles and stick them in position.

10 Stick a circle of plain colored paper over the nose on each side. Assemble the sausage dog by slotting in the ears, pushing the tube through for the wheels, and then attaching the wheels. The wheels should fit snugly but you should be able to adjust their position so that your dog will stand up.

Making the body

To achieve the thickness required for the body, I have created double-thick cardstock by sticking two sheets together, but this is quite hard work to cut out. Foamboard is thicker than cardstock and is much easier to cut.

Swinging monkeys mobile

Hanging mobiles look great in a child's bedroom. This cheery monkey mobile is fun and very adaptable—all the monkeys are made as individual pieces and can hang from each other, so you can create different shape mobiles. They will happily swing all together from the ceiling, or dotted separately around the room.

you will need:

Monkey template on page 166

Tracing paper

Pencil

20 x 20in. (50 x 50cm) foamboard

Scalpel or craft knife

Cutting mat

Glue stick

Sheets of patterned paper

Sheet of plain paper

Scissors

⅜in. (4mm) hole punch

Hammer

Length of string

1 Trace the monkey template and transfer the base shape onto a piece of thin foamboard. Cut out the shape.

2 Glue one side of the monkey and lay it down on the reverse side of one of the sheets of patterned paper. Trim around the edge using a scalpel or craft knife to remove the excess paper. Repeat to cover the other side.

3 Use the template to draw the face on the plain paper. Carefully cut out the face outline using scissors, and cut out the features using a scalpel or craft knife and the hole punch.

4 Stick the face down in position on the monkey. Make a few more monkeys in the same way. Punch a small hole in the top of one monkey and thread a length of string through to hang it. Suspend the other monkeys from the first.

Paper slippers

These beautifully decorative slippers would make a lovely gift for someone special. You can buy wonderful papers from all over the world—I have used some very special Japanese Chiyogami paper, which is screen-printed by hand in gorgeous colors and designs. It is expensive, but a sheet is quite large and you need only use small amounts to make stunning projects.

you will need:

Slippers template on page 166
Tracing paper
Pencil
Scalpel or craft knife
Cutting mat
Thin white cardstock
Glue stick
3 pieces of decorative paper
Scissors

Adhesive tape (optional)
Piece of thick colored paper
Piece of thin silver paper

1 Trace the templates for the sole, toe piece, and upper section and transfer them to the thin white cardstock. Cut out the shapes.

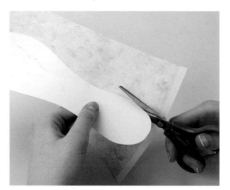

2 Stick down the upper section to the reverse side of one of the sheets of decorative paper and then cut around the shape. Do the same with the sole section.

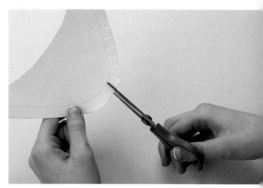

3 Using a pencil draw a line ⅜in. (1cm) in from the edge all around the curved front section of the upper shape. Cut down to this line all around in snips approx. ⅜in. (1cm) apart.

Paper know-how

These slippers are not intended to be worn long term—the paper is too delicate for them to last very long—although if you use sturdy paper, they could perhaps be worn once or twice for a very special occasion.

If you want to make the slipper to a particular size, match the size of the sole to another shoe of the right size, and then enlarge the other pieces to the same ratio.

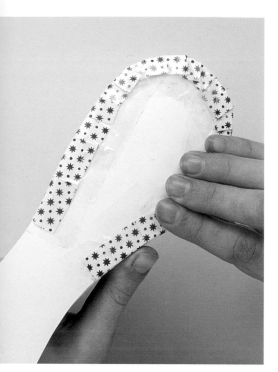

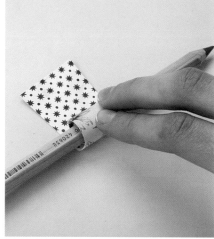

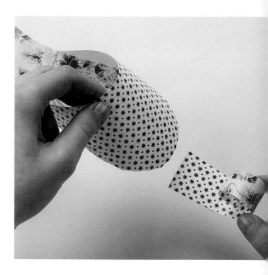

5 Cover both the front and back of the toe piece with patterned paper and then wrap it around a pencil to curl the end.

6 Add glue to the uncurled end of the toe piece and stick it to the underside of the front section of the sole.

4 Fold the snipped edge under. Glue along the edge and stick it to the plain underside of the front section of the sole. Make sure the ends line up and both sides are the same length. This part is tricky so you can use some adhesive tape as well to help stick the edge down.

7 Cut out a heel section from patterned paper and stick this in position at the back of the upper side of the sole.

8 Cut out another sole shape from the thick colored paper and stick this to the bottom of the slipper.

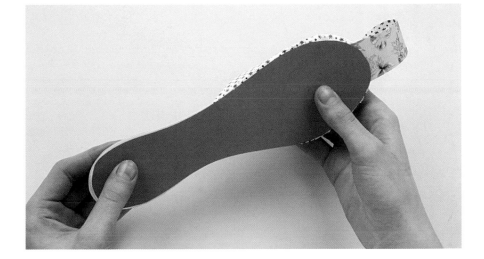

9 Cut two oblongs of silver paper 8 x 1½in. (20 x 4cm) and 8 x 2½in. (20 x 6cm). Cut a fringe along one long side of each piece. Make the cuts approx. ³⁄₁₆in. (4mm) apart and stop approx. ³⁄₈in. (1cm) from the other edge.

10 Glue along the bottom edge of the smaller fringe and roll up tightly. Glue along the bottom edge of the larger fringe and carry on rolling around the smaller one.

11 Hold the tassel in position on the front of the slipper, centered and approx. ⅞in. (2cm) from the edge. Draw around the base with a pencil.

12 Cut a slit at the mark with a craft knife across the circle and then another one to create a cross. Fluff up the tassel.

13 Dab a bit of glue onto the flaps of the cross and push the tassel down through them and approx. ⅜in. (1cm) into the hole. Repeat all the instructions again to make up the other slipper.

Slipper style

The curled toe and the tassel give these slippers a very Eastern look, but you can easily create a different style. Try omitting the curled toe and instead of the tassel add crepe paper flowers like those made for the paper chandelier on page 28.

Clothespin dolls

These little ladies are dressed beautifully in clothes made from a theater poster and vintage music scores with elegant script lettering. There is an old-fashioned look about them—perched among some pretty pieces of period china, they make a charming display.

you will need:

Scraps of theater poster and vintage music score

Scalpel or craft knife

Cutting mat

Glue stick

Wooden push-on-style clothespins

Masking tape

Scissors

Clothespin doll templates on page 167

Tracing paper

Pencil

Thin black and red felt-tip pens

1 Cut out from theater poster a 6¾ x 2¾in. (17 x 7cm) oblong for the dress and one 1¾ x 1½in. (4.5 x 3.5cm) for the hat. Make little folds along the top of the dress section to gather it.

2 Glue the dress along the top and wrap it around the peg, making sure the feet show. Secure around the top of the dress with a thin piece of masking tape.

3 For the arm section, cut out a 2 x ¼in. (5cm x 6mm) strip from the music score. Place a blob of glue in the center of the arm section and stick in position on the body.

Paper know-how

Try making the dolls more personal by adapting the clothes and the hat to make them similar to something the recipient would wear. You could also dress the dolls as the different characters in a fairy tale.

Here the hair has been drawn on the doll with a marker, but you could glue strands of colored wool to the head to create longer hair or braids. Add the wool before you put the hat in place—or use it in place of the hat.

Clothespin doll clips

Clothespin dolls do not have to be merely decorative—make one for each person in the house and use them to hold specific notes, letters, or lists. You could also use them as personal place markers at the table—the possibilities are endless!

4 Trace the templates and transfer the shawl and shoe pieces to the poster and cut out. Cut a fringe along the top edge of the shawl and wrap it around the top of the body, securing with a blob of glue.

5 Cut a fringe with scissors along the top edge of the hat piece, leaving about ¼in. (6mm) free to overlap. Glue and wrap the hat around the head.

6 Add the shoe pieces to the bottom tips of the pin. Draw the hair, nose, and eyes onto the head with black felt-tip pen and the lips and cheeks in red.

Hanging fruit

Whether you make individual hanging fruit or a pretty mixed fruit garland, the bright colors and evocative shapes of these apples and pears will add a touch of nature to your kitchen. A single fruit would also make an attractive gift tag.

you will need:

Fruit templates on page 167

Tracing paper

Pencil

Sheets of thick paper in contrasting colors

Scalpel or craft knife

Cutting mat

Paper twine

Masking tape

Glue stick

Sewing machine and thread

Soft eraser

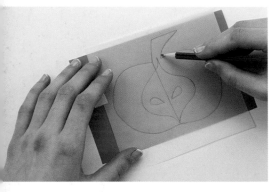

1 Trace the whole apple from the fruit templates and transfer the shape onto a piece of thick colored paper. Transfer a half apple shape to a contrasting color paper. Cut out the apple shapes.

2 Cut a piece of paper twine approx. 8in. (20cm) in length. Fold it in half and lay it vertically down the inside center of the whole apple. Secure with a small piece of masking tape, positioning the loop to one side of the stalk.

3 Turn the apple shape over so the twine is underneath and use a few dabs of glue to stick the half apple to cover one side of the whole apple.

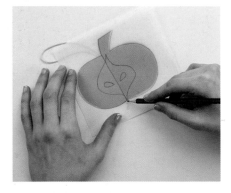

4 Trace the core shape and the pips from the template and transfer these lines onto the apple shape.

5 Using a sewing machine, stitch over the outline of the core. Use a soft eraser to rub out any pencil lines that still show.

6 Cut out the two pip shapes with the scalpel or craft knife. Repeat steps 1–6 for more apples and for the pears.

salud nature
saludable & natural

Pleated fan circles

I used to make these clever pleated circles every Christmas as a child, but I think they make wonderful decorations for any time of the year. They would look stunning made in gold and silver for a wedding party, for instance. You could also make smaller ones to decorate a gift instead of using ribbon bows.

you will need:

Sheets of giftwrap paper

Ruler

Short lengths of plastic-covered wire (as used to secure food storage bags)

Glue stick

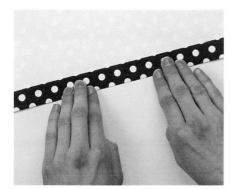

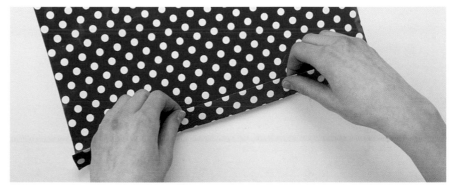

1 For the large size use two sheets of giftwrap paper. Take one of the sheets with the pattern facing down and fold over a ⅞in. (2cm) deep strip across the width of the paper.

2 Turn the paper over right side upward, with the end you are folding nearest you. Fold the ⅞in. (2cm) deep strip back the other way to make a pleated zigzag.

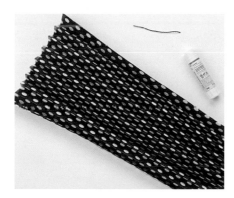

3 Continue to fold over a strip then turn the paper over and fold back until you reach the end and the entire sheet is pleated.

4 Fold the pleated strip in half and press firmly at the crease.

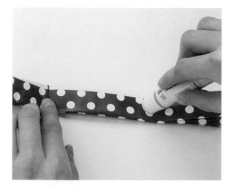

5 Secure with a short length of plastic-coated wire, wound around the crease and twisted to hold in place.

6 Open out the two halves of pleated paper and run the glue stick down the length of the outer strip on one half.

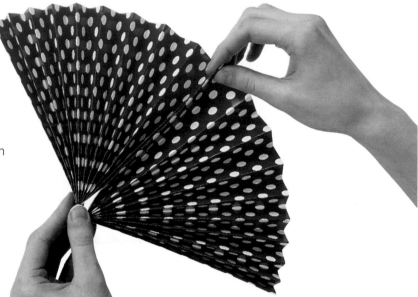

7 Fold the pleated paper in half again and stick the two halves together to make a semicircle. Repeat steps 1–7 to make the other half of the circle.

8 Run the glue stick down the edge of one semicircle and stick it to the edge of the other semicircle to make a complete circle. You should be gluing right side to right side— if your last folded strip facing outward is the inside of the giftwrap paper, you should trim this off.

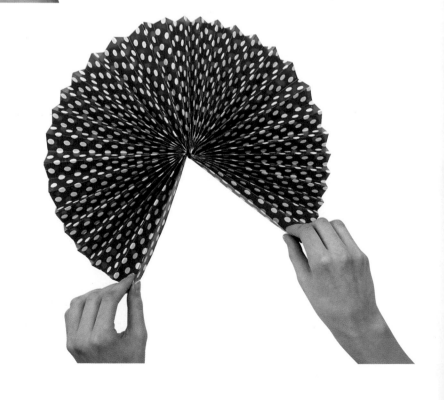

Paper know-how

Almost any design of patterned paper is effective for these fans, although it needs to be able to take a good, sharp crease. The paper should also be fairly stiff—floppy paper will not hold the circular shape required here.

chapter three

Gifts

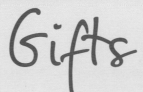

Gift boxes

The shape of these little gift boxes is reminiscent of the domes and finials often seen in Eastern architecture and I have chosen scraps of wallpaper to cover them to emphasize their rather exotic look. Tied with a pretty ribbon and filled with homemade candy, they would make a lovely gift.

you will need:

Piece of wallpaper or sheet of giftwrap paper

16 x 14in. (39 x 35cm) piece of thin cardstock

Glue stick

Box template on page 167

Tracing paper

Pencil

Scalpel or craft knife

Cutting board

¼in. (6mm) hole punch

Hammer

Bone folder

Length of ribbon

1 Stick down the piece of wallpaper or giftwrap paper onto the piece of thin cardstock.

2 Trace the box template and transfer the outline to the card.

3 Cut out the shape carefully with the scalpel and use the hole punch and hammer to make the four holes in the tabs. Cut the slots for the tabs.

4 Score the inner lines with the bone folder where indicated to create the box shape.

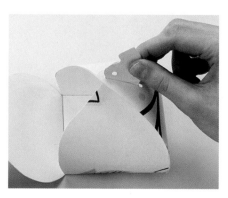

5 Place the two tabs with punched holes aligned and slot the other two sides into position.

6 Thread a ribbon through the holes and tie into a decorative bow to finish.

Notebooks

I use notebooks all the time and keep one in my bag to scribble down ideas. They make a great gift if you personalize them with photos or pictures. The owl pattern is printed with a stamp made from one of my drawings—many companies make up stamps, or you can buy one ready-made.

you will need:

14 sheets of letter size (A4) paper in a pale color such as white or cream

Sheet of letter size (A4) thin colored cardstock

Bone folder

Pencil

Ruler

Needle and strong thread

Hand-stamped sheet or picture of choice

Glue stick

Sheet of contrast color thin cardstock

Length of round elastic cord

Masking tape or clear adhesive tape

Scalpel or craft knife

Cutting mat

1 Fold approx. 14 sheets of letter size (A4) paper in half. Score down the center and fold the piece of thin letter size (A4) cardstock in half.

2 Place the sheets of paper together, with the cardstock on the outside as the cover. Open out and along the center fold make a series of pencil dots at 1¼-in. (3-cm) intervals.

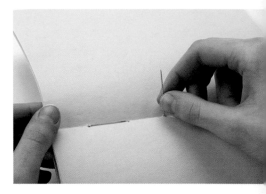

3 Knot the end of the thread in the needle. Bring the needle up through the spine from the outside to the inside at the first dot at the bottom. Go back down through the next dot and back up through the first hole again. Go back down the second hole and come up through the third hole.

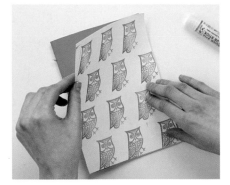

4 Repeat until you have reached the last dot to make a row of three stitches that have been stitched twice for strength. Tie off the thread and cut off the ends. Stick your chosen picture or print on the front of the book.

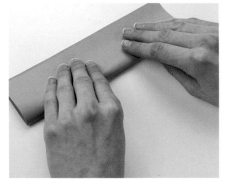

5 Cut out an oblong from the piece of contrast cardstock that is the same length as the book and 3¼in. (8cm) wide. Score and fold it in half.

6 Cut a piece of round elastic cord 12in. (30cm) in length and fold this in half. Make a hole in the center of the cardstock along the fold line and poke the folded end of the elastic through.

Using stamps

Stamping designs onto plain paper is a great way to make your own giftwrap and matching tags.

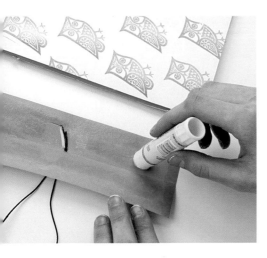

7 Secure the ends of the elastic on the inside of the folded cardstock with a small piece of masking tape or clear adhesive tape.

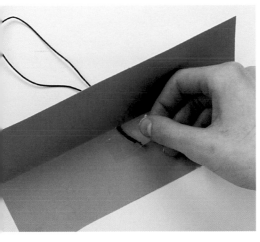

8 Glue the folded oblong over the spine of the notebook to finish. If the edges of the inside pages protrude from the cover, trim them off with the scalpel or craft knife.

Photo album

Although we live in a world where digital images are the norm, with hundreds of pictures on cameras and computers, it is still a great pleasure to look through a real photo album. Choose a selection of special images and display them in this handcrafted book, which is sure to become a family favorite and treasured for generations.

you will need:

Wavy template on page 167

Tracing paper

Soft pencil

2 erasers

Sharp pencil

Scalpel or craft knife

Cutting mat

Inkpads in two contrast colors

2 sheets of thin letter size
(A4) paper to print

2 sheets of letter size (A4)
thick cardstock

2 strips of bookbinders' cloth,
each 10½ x 4¾in. (26 x 12cm)

Glue stick

Metal ruler

Sheets of thick letter size (A4)
paper for album pages

22in. (56cm) of ½in. (12mm)
wide sewing tape

Double-sided tape

Double hole punch

¼in. (6mm) hole punch

Hammer

2 bookbinders' fasteners

1 Trace the template with a soft pencil. Press one eraser down onto the trace so that the pattern is transferred onto the eraser. Go over the lines with a sharp pencil, to make them clearer.

2 Use a scalpel or craft knife to cut away the background of the design, and the points in the wavy shape.

3 Press the block onto one of the inkpads and use it to print up the design onto the two pieces of thin paper.

4 Repeat steps 1–3 with the other eraser to print up the contrasting color on the same sheets of paper.

5 Measure and cut a 1½in. (4cm) wide strip from the end of one of the pieces of thick cardstock. Then trim a further ⅛in. (3mm) strip off the larger piece.

6 Fold a piece of the bookbinders' cloth in half. Glue the reverse side and lay the 1½in. (4cm) wide strip of cardstock centered and right side up next to the middle fold in the cloth. Position the larger piece of thick cardstock directly below this, leaving an ⅛in. (3mm) gap between the two. Press down firmly.

7 Align the metal ruler along the side edge of the cardstock and cut the cloth from the top edge down to the point of the cardstock. Align the ruler along the top of the cardstock and cut the cloth from the point of the cardstock to the right-hand edge; remove this oblong of cloth. Do the same on the other side.

8 Fold the top flap of the bookbinders' cloth over the cardstock, and then fold in the two side flaps. Press down firmly to stick.

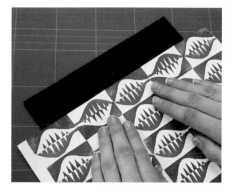

9 Glue the reverse of one of the printed-paper sheets. Center the paper so that it overlaps the cardstock evenly on both side edges, with the top edge lined up with the ⅛in. (3mm) gap between the two pieces of cardstock.

10 Turn the cardstock over. Cut two oblongs from the two corners of the paper where it extends past the card, as you did for the cloth in step 7. Turn the two side flaps in, and then fold the end flap over. Press down firmly to stick.

11 Repeat steps 6–10 to make the back cover—this time you do not need to divide the thick cardstock so there is no need to repeat step 5. Cut a short slit in both covers, in the center and ¾in. (18mm) in from the paper-covered edge.

12 Cut the length of sewing tape in half and thread one end through one of the covers from back to front. Secure the end inside with a piece of double-sided tape. Repeat on the other cover.

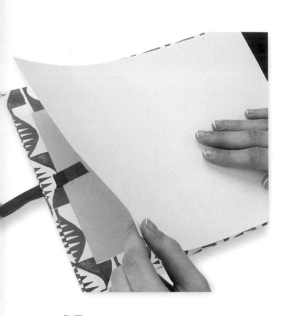

13 Trim two sheets of the thick letter size (A4) paper to 10½in. (26cm) and stick in place on the inside of the front and back covers.

14 Working on a few sheets at a time, center the double hole punch along one short end of the remaining sheets of thick paper and punch a pair of holes in all the inside pages.

15 Mark with a pencil where holes to match the inside pages should be on the front and back covers, and then use the single punch and hammer to make the holes.

16 Place the back section of the bookbinders' fasteners into the back cover. Add all the inside pages and then place the front cover in position and screw in the front section of the fastener.

Theme album

If you are making an album to hold photos of one special occasion, it can be a nice touch to create a cover design that reflects what is inside, or you could add a title panel to the front cover.

Pot and pencils

This is a project that the children can get involved with—it is so easy and very eco-friendly because, except for the pencils, everything is recycled. Although if your home is anything like mine, you probably have dozens of pencils hidden away in drawers waiting to be transformed! Use a variety of papers, such as giftwrap, old books, comics, maps, posters, or attractive labels. Make sure you have a good mix of colors and patterns.

you will need:

Pot or can to recycle
Metal ruler
Pencil
Sheets of patterned paper
Scalpel or craft knife
Cutting mat
Glue sticks
Pencils to cover

1 Find a suitable pot to cover—you need one around 4–5in. (10–12.5cm) high and 2–3in. (5–7.5cm) in diameter. Divide the height of your pot by three then add 1/8in. (3mm) for overlap. Measure the circumference of the pot and add 3/8in. (1cm) for overlap. Cut three oblongs to the final dimensions using different papers.

2 Stick the three oblongs, with each one slightly overlapping the next, around the pot.

3 Cut out another oblong the height of the pot and long enough to fit around the pot with 3/8in. (1cm) for overlap. Stick this down in position to line the inside of the pot.

4 Cut oblongs of paper the length of your pencils to the beginning of the sharpened part, and wide enough to wrap around the pencil with 1/4in. (5mm) overlap. Wrap the paper around the pencils and stick down.

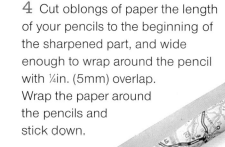

Handprinted wrap and tags

Creating unique giftwrap is easy with an eraser and some colored inkpads. Use a craft knife to cut out the design to make a stamp. After a bit of practice, you can experiment and will soon be printing your own sheets of paper to use for giftwrap and tags, and covering notebooks or pencil pots.

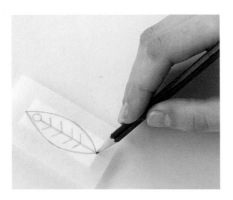  

1 Trace the template with a soft pencil. Press the eraser down onto the trace so that the pattern is transferred onto the eraser. Go over the lines with a sharp pencil, to make them clearer.

2 Use a scalpel or craft knife to cut away the background of the design, and the veins in the leaf shape.

3 Press the block onto an inkpad and use it to print up the design onto cardstock or paper.

4 Experiment with using different layouts and colors.

Creative print

The designs here were printed with the same stamp design using different colors. Using less ink gives a lighter color—press lightly onto the inkpad and paper, and print off excess ink onto a spare scrap of paper first. Use light and darker shades to add depth to the design.

Ribbon tie gift bags

Every one loves to receive homemade presents in the form of cookies, fudge, or brownies, and what better way of presenting them than in these gorgeous ribbon-tied gift bags? They look as if they have been bought at a very exclusive store rather than made from a spare piece of wallpaper and a scrap of ribbon.

you will need:

Giftwrap paper
Pencil
Metal ruler
Scalpel or craft knife
Cutting mat
Bone folder
Glue stick
8in. (20cm) length of ribbon

1 Take a piece of the paper and measure and cut out an oblong 13 x 9¼in. (32 x 23cm). On the reverse side of the paper, mark with a pencil at these measurements along the long top edge: 3¼in. (8cm), 1⅜in. (3.5cm), 1⅜in. (3.5cm), 3¼in. (8cm), 1⅜in. (3.5cm), 1⅜in. (3.5cm), and ⅞in. (2cm). Do the same along the bottom edge, or use a triangle (set square), then join the marks together to show where you score and fold the paper. Score all along the lines.

2 Start with the paper reverse side up and the ⅞in. (2cm) marked strip nearest to you. Fold the first strip over. The next fold along forms the center of the side panel, so turn the paper over and fold the other way.

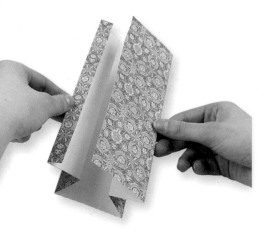

3 The next two folds form the edges of the back panel, then the following one folds in again to form the center of the other side. Carry on until you have folded all score lines to form the bag shape.

4 Align the fold on the ⅞in. (2cm) flap with the edge of the front panel and stick down. Mark a line 2in. (5cm) up from one end of the bag and score along it with the bone folder or the back of the knife. Fold the bag outward at this point on both sides to form the creases that will begin to create the base of the bag.

The right size bag

The finished bag is around 7in. (17.5cm) tall, but it can be shorter or taller to match your gift simply by making the shorter measurement of the initial oblong of paper either smaller or larger. For example, if you want a bag 4in. (10cm) tall, start with an oblong of paper 13 x 6¼in. (32 x 15.5cm).

5 Position the bag so that the front panel is facing you and the base of it is at the top. Gently crease a diagonal fold from one end of the cross fold made in step 4 up to the center of the uppermost edge of the bag.

6 Repeat on the other side of the front panel and then turn the bag around and do the same with the back panel.

7 Gently push and ease the folds at the side panels so that they fold in, leaving two folded triangles that you can now fold flat to form the base of the bag.

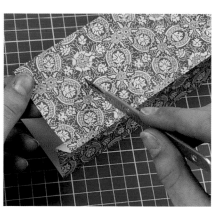

8 Glue along the inside of the bottom edge of the bag and under the two triangle flaps. Place one hand down inside the bag and press the glued flaps to form the base.

9 Make a small split at the center and about 1½in. (4cm) down from the top edge on the front and back sections of the bag.

10 Pull the length of ribbon through, leaving about ½in. (1cm) of ribbon on the inside. Glue a small disk of paper over the end of the ribbon to hold securely.

Paper beads

When you wear this beaded necklace, people will not believe that it is made from simple scraps of paper. I have used a stripy metallic giftwrap paper here, but try experimenting with alternative types of paper to create very different-looking beads.

you will need:

Triangle bead templates on page 168

Pencil

Tracing paper

Sheets of thin colored paper such as giftwrap

Metal ruler

Scalpel or craft knife

Cutting mat

Toothpick or thick needle

Glue stick

Sewing needle

Reel of waxed beading thread or strong thread for stringing beads

Liquid adhesive

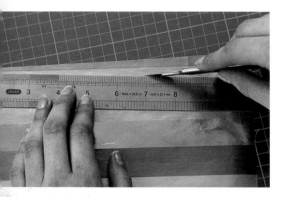  

1 Measure or trace the bead templates and transfer them to the thin colored paper. Cut out several long triangles, one for each bead.

2 Wind the paper triangle tightly around the toothpick or thick needle, starting at the wide end.

3 Around ¼in. (6mm) before the end, place a dab of glue on the tip of the triangle and then carry on winding to the end.

4 Slide the bead off the needle, then make a few more beads in different sizes. Cut a 26in. (65cm) length of waxed thread and start to thread the beads onto it using the sewing needle.

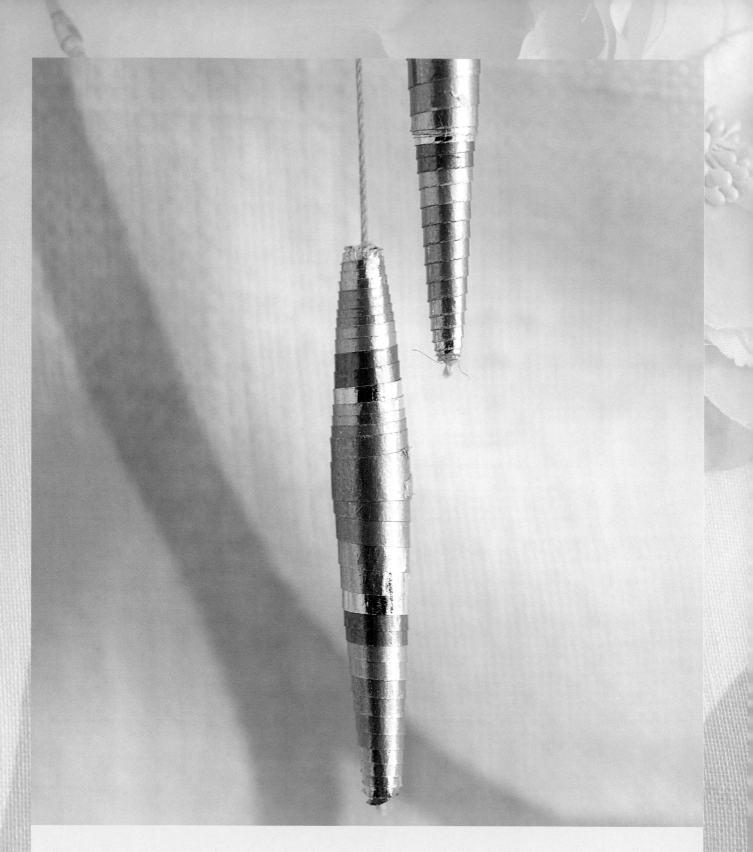

Keeping up appearances

Paper beads are not waterproof and are fairly delicate, so over time they may start to become a little tatty around the edges. A coat of clear lacquer will help to protect them—alternatively, just make yourself some new ones!

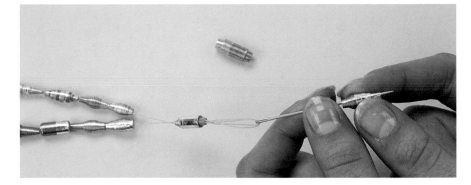
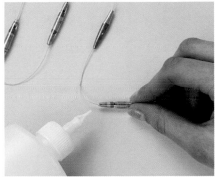

5 At the center of the necklace, leave a gap of about 3¼in. (8cm), then carry on adding beads. Knot the thread ends together to secure when you have finished adding beads. Fold the length of unbeaded thread in the center of the necklace in half and thread it through the needle. Thread some beads onto this double piece of thread, leaving approx. ⅜in. (1cm) clear at the end.

6 Cut another piece of waxed thread approx. 12in. (30cm) in length. Leaving random length gaps between each bead, thread on several beads. As you position each bead, place a dab of liquid adhesive on the thread and slide the bead over this to secure in place.

7 Thread the second beaded length through the loop at the base of the short row of beads at the center of the necklace. Stagger the two sides so that one side is approx. 8in. (20cm) and the other side is approx. 4in. (10cm). Make up two more lengths of beads as in step 6, both approx. 8in. (20cm) long. Thread them through the loop as before, again staggering the lengths on each side.

8 Place a dab of liquid adhesive on the bottom of the last bead on the short row of beads at the center of the necklace and push it down tight against the hanging threads of beads to hold them secure.

Dragonfly clothespins

I find these charming little clips very useful for keeping things like receipts, bills, and letters organized. They are simplicity itself to make, and children will love creating them—you could try other insects like ladybugs, butterflies, or bumblebees as well.

you will need:

Dragonfly template on page 168
Pencil
Tracing paper
Scraps of brightly colored paper
Scissors
Glue stick
Wooden clothespins
Beads, buttons, or glitter sequins (optional)

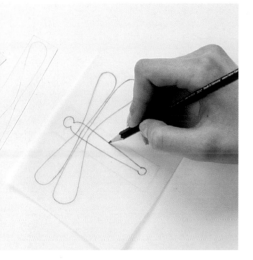

1 Trace the dragonfly template. Transfer the body shape to the reverse of a piece of colored paper.

2 Transfer the two wings to contrasting paper and then cut out all the shapes.

3 Stick the two pairs of wings in place, then stick the body over the wings down the length of the clothespin.

Tips

Try using these as clips on plain paper bags to create original and unusual party bags. They would also be a great project to make at a kids' craft party—I have held many a craft-themed party for my children and they are always the ones that run the smoothest!

If you are using this as a project for children, they may enjoy sticking beads, buttons, sequins, and glitter onto the insect body. I have used a shiny paper from a craft store for some dragonfly sparkle.

Silver leaf fish

I have always loved using silver leaf in paper projects; it adheres completely to become part of the paper surface, and the imperfections of gaps and scratches are all part of the appeal. Each time you use it, you create something individual and unique. Lean these fish against the wall to make stunning art pieces that will sparkle and glimmer in the changing light.

you will need:

3 square sheets of silver leaf

Scissors

Approx. 10 x 24in. (25 x 60cm) piece of blue paper

Pencil

Size (special liquid glue for silver leaf)

Fish template on page 168

Tracing paper

Scalpel or craft knife

Cutting mat

12 x 24in. (30 x 60cm) brown cardstock

Length of thick cardstock

Glue stick

⁵⁄₁₆in. (7mm) hole punch

Hammer

1 Cut the three squares of silver leaf in half with the scissors to make six triangles.

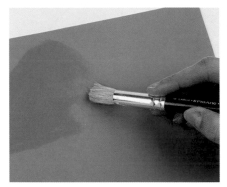

2 Lay one of the triangles onto the blue paper with the point centered at the top. Very lightly with a pencil mark the area of the triangle. Center the triangle again directly under the first and mark this area, continuing down the length to mark six triangles. Brush size into the marked triangles.

3 Wait a few moments for the size to dry a little and then lay a triangle of the silver leaf face down onto it, with the backing paper facing up. Rub down gently and then carefully remove the backing paper.

4 Trace the template and transfer the fish shape onto the blue paper, centered over the row of silver triangles. Transfer the position of the eye from the template.

5 Cut out the fish shape. Lay a piece of tracing paper over the silver leaf to smooth down the triangles firmly.

6 For the other fish design, transfer the fish shape to the brown cardstock and cut out.

7 Cut triangles of different sizes from the leftover blue paper from the first fish. These can be random sizes but keep them all within a height measurement of 3¼in. (8cm). Starting 7¼in. (18cm) down from the top of the fish, draw a pencil line across the width. Draw one every 3¼in. (8cm) until you reach the tail. Stick the triangles along the lines, varying the heights but keeping the base of each triangle on the line. Cut three thin triangles approx. 2in. (5cm) in length for the tail section.

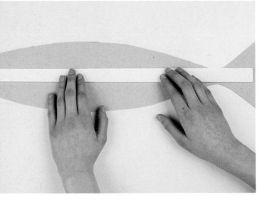

8 Cut two strips of thick cardstock slightly shorter than the fish and around ½in. (12mm) wide and stick to the reverse of each fish to stiffen them.

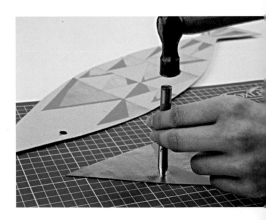

9 Using the hole punch and hammer, make a hole in the head of each fish for the eye.

Paper know-how

Silver leaf doesn't just have to used with card or paper. You can also use it to decorate other objects, like these attractive round pebbles that look great when dispayed with the fish.

Flower fridge magnets

These cute and colorful magnets are ideal to stick on the refrigerator or other metal surface to keep control of all those pieces of paper that seem to build up so quickly in our hectic day-to-day lives. Or use them to display your children's pictures, or a collection of postcards, for an ever-changing art exhibit.

you will need:

Disk magnet
Scraps of origami paper in two designs
Pencil
Scissors
Glue stick
Ruler

1 Draw around the magnet onto one of the pieces of paper. Cut out the circle and stick it to the front of the magnet.

2 Cut an oblong in contrasting paper, 1½in. (4cm) in depth, wrap it around the magnet, and cut off a length to match the circumference. Fold the oblong in half with the pattern on the outside.

3 Snip a fringe all the way along the folded edge of the oblong, making the snips approx. ⅛in. (3mm) deep. Stop approx. ¼in. (6mm) from the edge.

4 Open the fold slightly and glue along the edge to join the two sides together. Glue along the bottom edge on one side and stick the fringe around the magnet.

5 Cut another oblong in the same paper the same length and 3in. (8cm) in depth and make a fringe as before, but making cuts approx. ¼in. (5mm) deep this time. Stick this fringe around the magnet over the base of the smaller one.

6 To finish, press down gently on the top of the fringes to open up the petals.

presents ple

chapter four
Cards

Russian doll card

Traditional little wooden nesting dolls from Russia have inspired this folding card. I was given a set as a child, which I still have, and I have always been charmed by the pretty folk designs painted on the wood. Single dolls would make enchanting gift tags—try scraps of folksy giftwrap paper to complete the look.

you will need:

Doll template on page 168

Pencil

Tracing paper

12 x 5in. (30 x 12.5cm) thin white cardstock

Scissors

Scraps of a variety of patterned papers

Glue stick

Scraps of plain colored paper for the faces

Scalpel or craft knife, or fine felt-tip pen

Cutting mat

Bone folder

1 Photocopy the doll template four times, reducing the size by 8% each time. Trace the templates, making sure that each size is butted right up alongside the next in line so that they are touching down one side.

2 Transfer the outline of the row of dolls onto the piece of thin cardstock. Cut out the entire row, keeping the dolls joined together.

3 Use the individual shapes on the templates to cut out the different size body shapes and headpieces from the patterned paper.

4 Stick down the relevant body shape, and then the headpiece, onto each doll in the row of dolls.

Getting the right look

Making the dolls in different paper gives each one a more individual look. However, in traditional nesting dolls of this type all the individual dolls in a set are identical—just gradually smaller in size—so you can use the same paper for each doll if you prefer.

5 Trace the oval for each face onto plain paper. Use the templates to draw the faces, then either use a scalpel to cut out the faces or draw them on with a fine felt-tip pen.

6 Color in the hair on the face section, or cut out the hair shape for each doll and stick it down. Stick each face onto its relevant body.

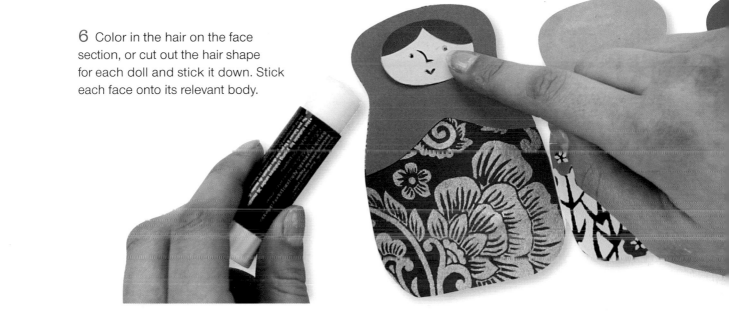

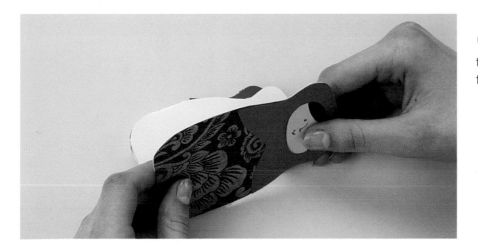

7 Score down where each doll joins the next. Fold the dolls back and forward to make a concertina shape.

Vintage shoe card

I keep all scraps of wallpaper left over from decorating and use them in many of my paper projects. For this shoe I have used a lovely vintage floral design; using different patterns will change the whole look of the card. Add pretty ribbon as a finishing touch.

you will need:

Sheet of tabloid size (A3) thin white cardstock

Scalpel or craft knife,

Cutting mat

Pencil

Metal ruler

Shoe template on page 169

Tracing paper

Scrap of patterned paper

Glue stick

Scrap of plain colored paper

⅜in. (4mm) hole punch

Hammer

Length of ribbon

1 Cut out a piece of white cardstock measuring 7 x 14in. (17.5 x 35cm). Use a knife to score down the center of the oblong halfway along the long edge then fold in half. Trace the template onto the patterned paper and cut out the shoe shape.

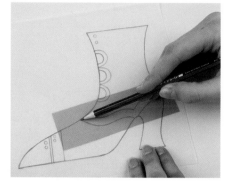

2 Use the template to cut out with a knife the decorative parts of the shoe from the plain colored paper. Punch holes where indicated.

3 Stick all the decorative parts down in position on the shoe.

4 Stick the shoe to the bottom half of the white cardstock at the center and approx ⅜in. (1cm) up from one short edge.

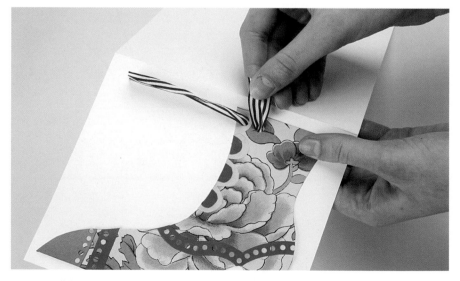

5 Punch two holes at the top of the shoe and thread a ribbon through. Tie the ribbon in a bow to complete.

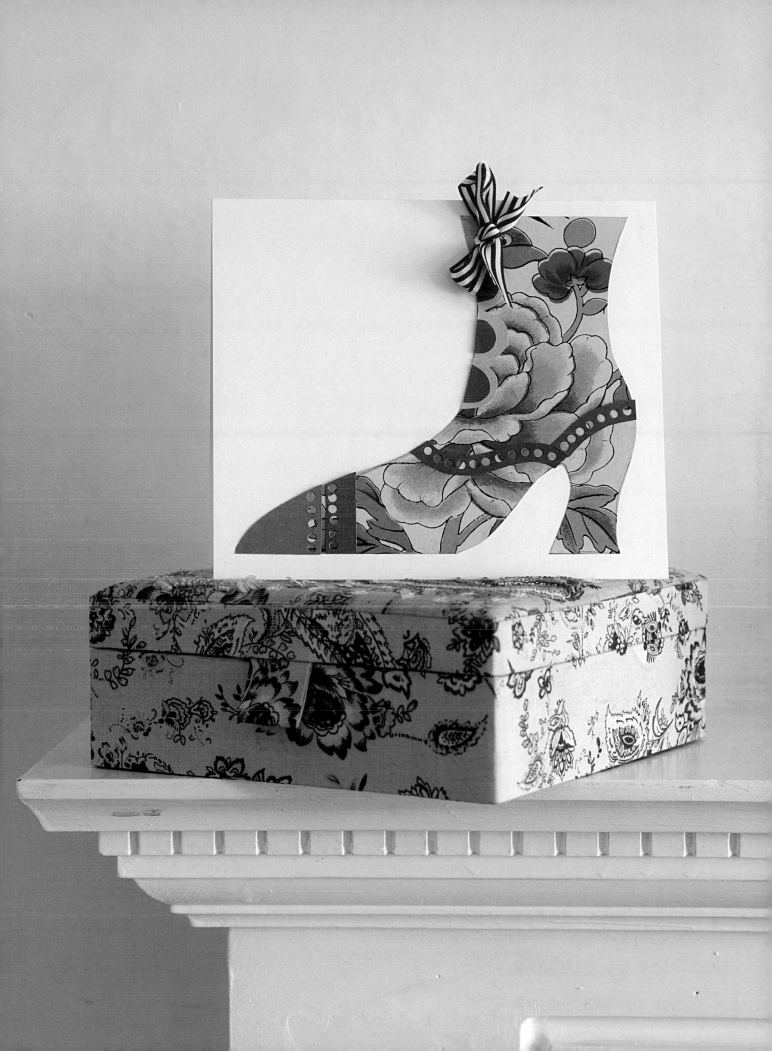

Vintage fold-out flower card

This pretty greetings card has the added surprise of opening up to display a beautiful 3-d flower, inside which is the perfect place to write a secret message!

you will need:

6 x 12in. (15 x 30cm) thin patterned cardstock

Glue stick

Flower template on page 169

Tracing paper

Pencil

Scissors

Bone folder

Sheets of patterned paper in two different designs

6 x 12in. (15 x 30cm) thin white cardstock

Cutting mat

Metal knife

Scalpel or craft knife

1 Cut out two pieces of thin patterned cardstock each 5½ x 5½in. (14 x 14cm). Stick together back to back.

2 Trace the large flower template and transfer all the lines to one side of the cardstock.

3 Cut out around the outline of the folding flower shape.

4 Score along the base of each petal where indicated and fold in.

5 Trace the small flower template and transfer the shape to one of the patterned papers. Cut out the shape and stick in the center of the folding flower. Fold up the flower, overlapping each petal and tucking the last petal underneath the first to secure.

Fold-out flower tag

This design would make a really great gift tag—just make up the front section of the card with its fold-out flower in the same way. You can write a personal message to the recipient, hidden underneath the folded petals.

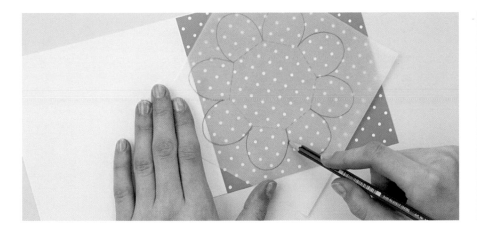

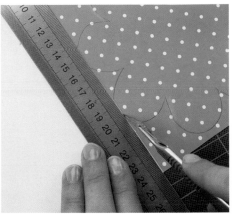

6 Cut out a piece of white cardstock 5½ x 11in. (14 x 28cm). Stick a square of contrasting patterned paper measuring 5½ x 5½in. (14 x 14cm) on the right-hand side of the cardstock. Trace out the large flower shape onto the patterned paper, moving the trace over by approx. ¼in. (6mm) so that the ends of two of the petals on the left-hand side are overlapping the center line. This is so that when you cut away the flower shape, the front of the card is still attached to the back section by these two petals.

7 Score down the center of the oblong of cardstock, along the edge of the pattern section, and fold the card in half.

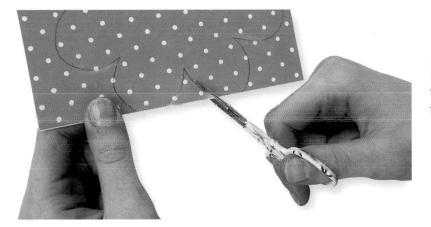

8 Cut out the flower shape through both layers of the cardstock, leaving the back and front still attached together by the ends of the two petals.

9 Stick the folded flower section into the center of the flower card.

Envelopes

The finishing touch to any homemade card is a stylish envelope—it seems a shame to put your beautiful creations in plain envelopes when it is so simple to create a matching design. These instructions are for an envelope to take the vintage fold-out flower card on page 110, but you can adapt them to any size card you want to make.

you will need:

Envelope template on page 169
Tracing paper
Pencil
Metal ruler
Sheet of patterned paper
Scalpel or craft knife
Cutting mat
Bone folder
Glue stick

1 Trace the template and transfer the envelope shape onto the sheet of patterned paper.

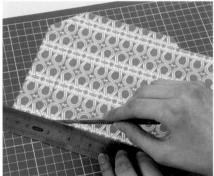

2 Cut out the envelope shape.

3 Score down each side tab and across the width at the base of the tabs using a bone folder or the back of the knife.

Size matters

To make the envelope for a different size card, measure the front of the card and add ¼in. (5mm) all around. Make up a template by using these measurements for the front and back sections only. Follow the width measurements from the original template to make up the side flaps, top flaps, and cut-away at the top of the envelope.

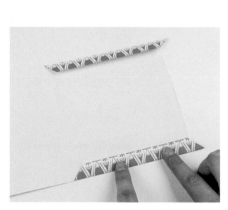

4 Fold in each side flap, fold the envelope in half, and then glue and stick the tabs in position.

5 Score and fold down the top flap.

Mini bunting card

I love the sight of bunting fluttering in the breeze—it instantly makes you think of warm summer days. This card will create a little of that summer feeling even on the gloomiest of winter evenings. You could also make a long string of bunting to tie around a gift to give it a stylish and original look.

you will need:

Piece of thin white cardstock

Thick colored paper

Scalpel or craft knife

Metal ruler

Cutting mat

Bunting template on page 169

Tracing paper

Pencil

Small scraps of bright colored paper

Scissors

Glue stick

Thin string

Needle

Masking tape

Bone folder (optional)

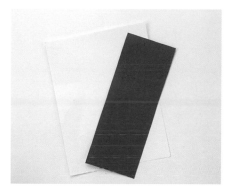

1 Cut out a piece of white cardstock 8 x 4in. (20 x 10cm) and a piece of colored paper 2 x 4in. (5 x 10cm).

2 Use the template to cut out one triangle in tracing paper. Using this as a template, hold scraps of paper against it and cut around to make up the bunting flags.

3 Fold over the flap at the top of one of the bunting triangles. Glue and fold the flap over a piece of thin string. Repeat until you have six flags in a row.

4 Use the needle to make a small hole in the top right- and left-hand corners of the piece of colored paper.

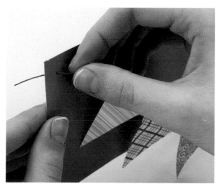

5 Thread the end of the string through the hole and secure on the reverse with a small piece of tape. Repeat with the other end.

6 Fold the white cardstock in half. You can use a bone folder to make a nice sharp fold, but it is not essential. Glue the reverse side of the colored paper and stick it to the front of the card.

Retro owl card

The owl is a popular design image at the moment, on fabric, giftwrap paper, clothes, or china. Use up scraps of bright paper in contrasting colors and patterns to make these charming owls. For the eyes, try to find scraps of paper with circular designs—flowers make great eyes and complete the retro 70s look.

you will need:

Owl template on page 170
Pencil
Tracing paper
Cutting mat
Metal ruler
6 x 12in. (15 x 30cm) thin white cardstock
Bone folder
Scissors

Sheets of patterned paper
Glue stick

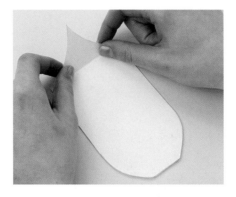

1 Use the template to transfer the design for the owl base shape onto the white cardstock, and cut out.

2 Score where indicated. Fold down the beak section and fold the owl card in half.

3 Using the template, cut out the beak, eyes, and wings from a selection of patterned paper.

4 Cut out the front piece of the owl from patterned paper and stick in position on the card. Add the wings, eyes, and beak.

Seahorse wrap and tags

The stylized cutout seahorse adds a real nautical touch to this giftwrap and matching tag, which is emphasized by the greens and blues used. If you are really short of time, just make up the tag and use purchased giftwrap paper in suitable watery colors.

you will need:

Seahorse tag template on page 170

Pencil

Tracing paper

Small piece of thin white cardstock

Metal ruler

Scalpel or craft knife

Cutting mat

Sheet of colored paper

Glue stick

⅛in. (4mm) hole punch

Hammer

Short length of thin ribbon

Wave template on page 170

Eraser

Inkpads in blue and green

Plain paper or giftwrap to print

1 Trace the template for the tag and the cutout design and transfer it to the thin white cardstock. Cut out the seahorse design from the cardstock using a scalpel or craft knife.

2 Stick the tag onto a slightly larger piece of colored paper.

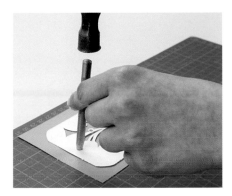

3 Punch a hole centered at the top of the tag to take the ribbon.

4 Trim the backing paper off level with the edge of the tag.

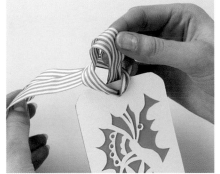

5 Thread the tie ribbon through the hole.

6 Follow the instructions for the hand-printed giftwrap project on page 84 to make the wave rubber stamp. Print the giftwrap paper in blues and greens.

Birdcage card

The bird motif is used frequently in most aspects of decorative art. Many of my designs include birds because these little feathered creatures make an enchanting image. This one, in a pretty, paper-cut bird cage, is special. It takes a more time than some cards in this book, but the effort is well worth it and you may want to keep it for yourself!

you will need:

6 x 7in. (15 x 17.5cm) thin blue cardstock

Scalpel or craft knife

Metal ruler

Cutting mat

Sheet of white letter size (A4) paper

Cage template on page 170

Pencil

Tracing paper

Scissors

Glue stick

12 x 7in. (30 x 17.5cm) thin white cardstock

Bird template on page 170

Small sheet of patterned paper

Length of thread

³⁄₁₆in. (4mm) hole punch

Hammer

Masking tape

Bone folder

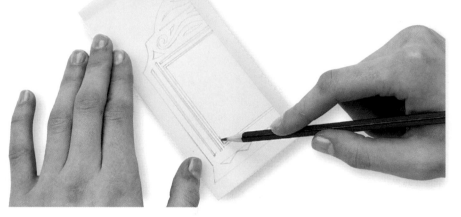

1 Cut out a piece of thin blue cardstock for the front of the card measuring 5½ x 6in. (14 x 15cm). Take a piece of white paper 5¼ x 5in. (13.5 x 12.5cm) and fold it in half. Trace the template for the cage and draw out the shape and the cutouts on the paper.

2 Cut out the marked areas on the white paper and open the cage out flat.

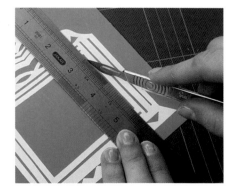

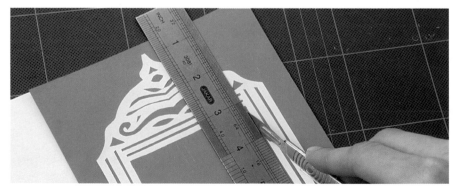

3 Center the cage on the piece of blue cardstock and stick down. Cut out an oblong of thin white cardstock 11 x 6in. (28 x 15cm).

4 Place the piece of blue cardstock on the right-hand half of the oblong, lining up the edges, but don't stick it down. Cut out the center section of the cage completely, cutting through both the blue layer and the white cardstock layer beneath, but leaving a small border of blue around the opening.

Adding movement

Suspending the bird on thread within the opening of the cage means it is free to swing around a little. Adding movement and a more 3-d look to your designs is a great way to make them look more complex than they really are. This card may take a little more time, but the techniques are simple.

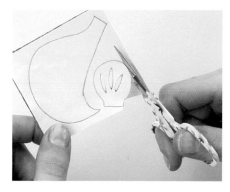 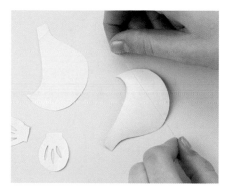 

5 Trace the bird template and cut out the front of the bird and the wing from white paper. Turn the tracing over to cut the back of the bird and the wing from the patterned paper.

6 Cut a 4in. (10cm) length of thread and center it down the middle of the bird.

7 Stick the front and back section of the bird together, sandwiching the thread in between the two layers.

8 Use the small hole punch to cut out the bird's eye. Score and fold over a ³⁄₁₆in. (4mm) flap on both wings and stick them in position on either side of the bird.

9 Center the bird in the cutout section of the white cardstock and secure each end of the thread on the front of the card with a little masking tape. Stick the blue cardstock piece to the front of the card, aligning the edges of the cutout.

10 Score down the middle of the oblong, along the edge of the blue cardstock piece, with the back of the scalpel blade or the bone folder. Fold the card in two to finish.

Button nest card

Small buttons make a lovely embellishment for homemade cards. Pearl buttons like these can be expensive to buy, but look out for them in thrift stores and flea markets. I was lucky to find two cushions covered in pearl buttons, which I have used for many projects. I also used old music scores and labels for the little bird to give the card a real vintage feel.

you will need:

18 x 12in. (45 x 30cm) thin blue cardstock

Pencil

Metal ruler

Scalpel or craft knife

Cutting mat

Robin, nest, leaves, and twigs templates on page 171

Tracing paper

Selection of small buttons

Sewing needle and thread

Sheets of printed and colored paper

1 Cut out a piece of cardstock for the front section of the card 5½ x 5½in. (14 x 14cm). Trace the nest template and use it to mark out the area for the nest.

2 Sew buttons onto the piece of cardstock to fill in the drawn outline of the nest shape.

3 Trace the relevant templates and transfer the outlines to interesting areas of the printed paper, then cut out the robin, leaves, and twigs. Cut the breast from a piece of red paper.

Stitching skills

Sewing the buttons on is very simple—first thread the needle and knot the end. Bring the needle up through the cardstock and one hole of a button, then take it down through the other hole. Move straight on to the next button—don't bother to fasten off the thread between each one.

Using buttons

A tiny button could be used here for the bird's eye, either sewn in place or glued. Adding buttons is a great way to quickly add interest and texture to your designs, so look out for other instances where you could substitute a button for a plain paper circle.

4 Stick down the robin, breast, twigs, and leaves in position on the front section of the card.

5 Cut out an oblong of cardstock 5½ x 11in. (14 x 28cm). Stick the decorated front section to the right-hand side of the oblong cardstock.

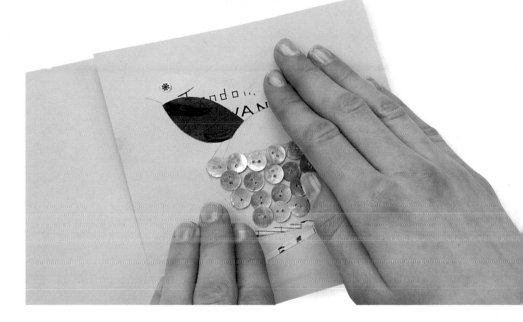

6 Score down the center of the oblong with the back of the scalpel at the edge of the decorated section and fold it over to complete the card.

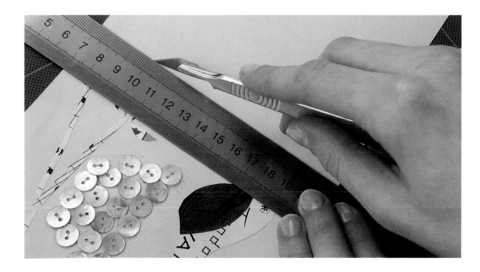

Filigree flower gift tag and card

For this project I was inspired by the beautiful designs of Japanese kimono fabrics. Use simple white cardstock for the outer section and pretty Japanese paper in bright citrus colors for the inside, to create a card and matching tag that are truly stunning.

you will need:

2 sheets 13 x 7in. (32.5 x 17.5cm) thin white cardstock

Pencil

Metal ruler

Cutting mat

Scalpel or craft knife

Filigree template for card on page 171

Tracing paper

Bone folder

Sheets of contrasting Japanese paper or giftwrap

Glue stick

Filigree template for tag on page 171

³⁄₁₆in. (4mm) hole punch

Hammer

Length of thin ribbon

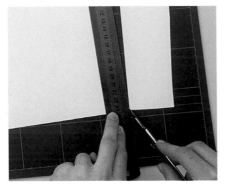

1 Measure and cut out an oblong 12¼ x 6⅛in. (31 x 15.5cm) from thin white cardstock.

2 Trace the template of the filigree cutout design onto the right-hand side of the oblong piece of cardstock.

3 Use a scalpel or craft knife to cut out the design.

4 Score down the middle of the cardstock and fold.

Keep it neat

The key to successful cutouts is to work slowly and carefully so you keep the apertures as neat and perfect as possible for a really professional-looking finish. Very untidy cutting or frayed edges can quickly spoil the effect.

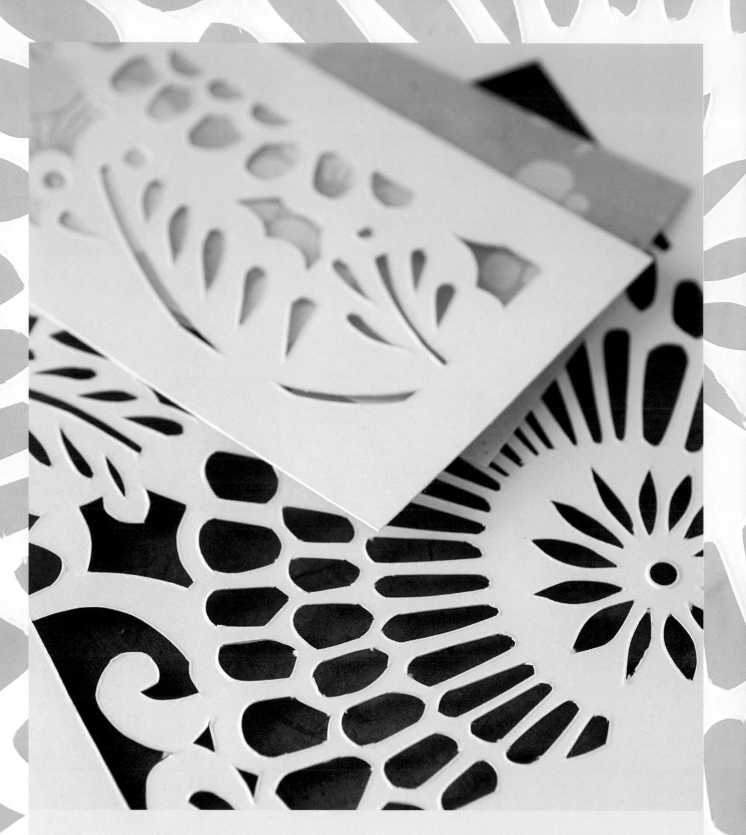

Coordinating designs

Items do not have to be identical to work well together—they just need to share some feature, whether this is design, color, or shape. This card and the gift tag have very different backing colors for extra zing but the cutout designs both use similar elements, which adds a coordinating factor.

5 Cut out a piece of colored paper 6⅛ x 6⅛in. (15.5 x 15.5cm) and stick in position on the inside of the card.

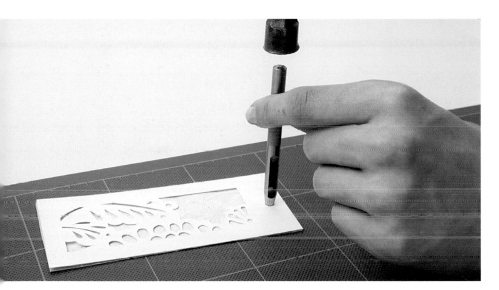

6 Measure and cut out a piece of thin white cardstock measuring 5¼ x 2¼in. (13.5 x 5.5cm). Trace the tag filigree design onto the cardstock and cut out. Cut out a piece of colored paper the same size as the tag, line up, and stick under the filigree design. Punch a hole ⅜in. (1cm) down from the top edge in the center.

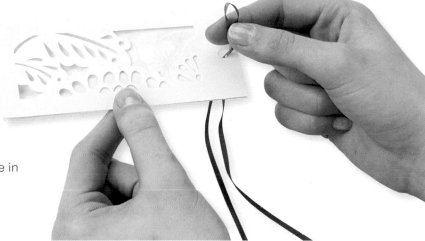

7 Attach a ribbon through the hole in the gift tag to finish.

chapter five
Party time

Vintage floral cakestand

There is something very charming about a table set for a real traditional tea, with an elegant tiered cakestand displaying a tempting selection of little cakes. I have used floral giftwrap paper and scraps of wallpaper in an old-fashioned style to complete the vintage look.

you will need:

Cakestand templates on page 172

Tracing paper

Pencil

24 x 17in. (60 x 42cm) piece of foamboard

Metal ruler

Scalpel or craft knife

Cutting mat

Quick-drying strong glue

Sheets of giftwrap paper or wallpaper

⅛in. (3mm) hole punch

⁵⁄₁₆in. (7mm) hole punch

Hammer

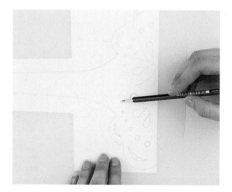

1 Trace the templates and transfer the central spine of the cakestand to a piece of foamboard, then cut out the shape.

2 Stick the central spine piece down on the reverse of your chosen paper. Cut around the board with a craft knife, and then repeat to cover the reverse side.

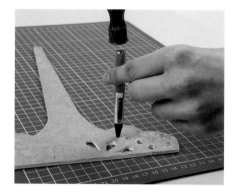

3 Use the template to transfer the cutout design on the base of the spine. Use a craft knife and the hole punches to cut out the design.

4 Use the templates to cut the two other side sections of the base from foamboard. Cover them and cut out the design as for the base of the central spine.

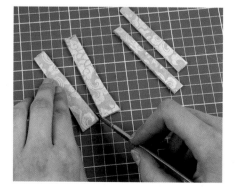

5 Cut out the remaining four sections of the central support from foamboard and cover these pieces in paper in the same way.

Choosing the right paper

Since the cakestand is to be used for food, there is always a danger of spills. Try using wipe-clean wallpaper for this project, so minor mishaps can be cleaned up easily.

6 Use the templates to cut out the circles for the tiers from foamboard and to mark the slots in the center of each circle. Cut out the slots using a craft knife. Cover the tiers with contrasting patterned paper in the same way as for the central spine.

7 Glue the top edges of the two side sections of the base. Slide the large circle onto the central spine so that it rests against the base. Hold it in position until the glue dries a little.

8 Glue the straight edges of the two largest central support sections and stick them on either side of the central spine, making sure everything stands flat and the two small sections are at right angles. Hold for a minute to let the glue dry a little.

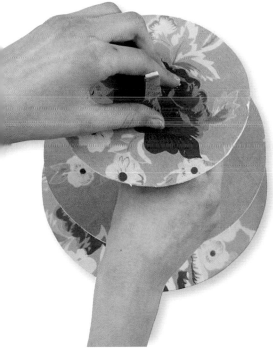

9 Add the medium circle, then the two smaller central support sections, and then the smallest circle in the same way.

10 Finally, cut out two circles from patterned paper and stick them either side of the top of the central spine to form a handle.

Cupcake toppers

There is a real craze for making cupcakes; even at weddings it is now not unusual to have tiers of beautifully decorated mini cakes instead of one traditional iced cake. These little cake toppers are such fun for a child's party and are easy to make using just scraps of paper. Try little ghosts for Halloween, flowers, footballs, flags—really the design possibilities are endless!

you will need:

Topper templates on page 173
Tracing paper
Pencil
Scraps of colored paper
Scissors
Toothpicks
Glue stick

1 Trace the templates and transfer the outlines onto several scraps of colored paper.

2 Cut out the flag and sail and two matching pieces for the hull section of each boat. Fold the flag and sail shapes in half.

3 Stick the flag and sail in position at the top of the toothpick, with the toothpick between the folded layers.

4 Stick the back and front sections of the hull on either side of the toothpick below the sail. Add the topper to your cup cake.

Geometric bunting

You can use simple triangles of scrap recycled paper to make lovely bunting, but I have added an extra twist by creating this design based on the British Union Jack flag. Festoon a patio for a summer barbecue or string some up in a child's bedroom for an original decoration.

you will need:

Geometric bunting template on page 173

Pencil

Tracing paper

Transparent plastic ruler

Sheets of white drawing (cartridge) paper

Scalpel or craft knife

Metal ruler

Cutting mat

Pieces of printed paper from comics, magazines, postcards, maps, packaging

Glue stick

Bone folder

Length of string

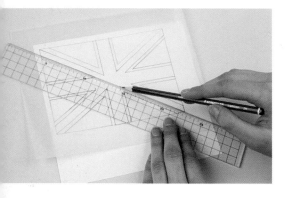

1 Trace the template and draw up the central cross shape and the two inner triangles, one large and one small, onto some drawing (cartridge) paper. Cut these out to use as a template to draw around.

2 Cut out an oblong of white drawing (cartridge) paper measuring 5¼ x 6¼in. (13 x 15.5cm) for each flag. Then draw around the cross template onto a piece of the printed paper.

3 Cut out the shape using a metal ruler and a scalpel or craft knife. If you are using the same paper for the triangle sections, try to keep the shape intact, so that if there is an all-over design, you can cut the triangles from the correct area.

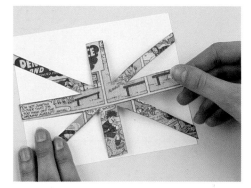

4 Stick the cross section down onto the white paper, lining up the bottom of the flag with the bottom of the paper.

5 Cut out the triangles from the correct segment of printed paper. The easiest way to do this is to hold the template against the paper and cut around it. If you prefer, you can vary the colors by cutting the cross from one color and the triangles from another.

6 Stick the triangle templates down in the corresponding areas of the flag to make up the rest of the design. Follow the guide to see where the large and small triangles fit, but you do not have to be too fussy about getting all the gaps even.

7 Score along the top of the flag image with a bone folder or the back of the scalpel and fold over the flap.

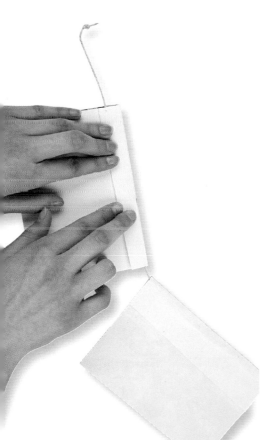

8 Glue along the flap and fold it over the length of string. Make several flags in the same way and space them out evenly along the string to make the bunting any length required.

Paper roses

I absolutely love these roses... I chose the brightest pink and orange crepe paper I could find. I have a huge bunch of them standing on a 1950s dressing table, where they look perfect in a retro, beautifully kitsch kind of way! You will need proper florists' wire and tape for this project.

you will need:

Rose petal template on page 173

Tracing paper

Pencil

Crepe paper in bright flower colors and green

Scissors

Leaf template on page 173

Glue stick

Florists' wire

Florists' tape

1 Trace the templates for the petal and draw out the shape onto the crepe paper. For one rose cut out 14 petals—you can cut more than one layer of crepe paper for several petals each time.

2 Repeat the same process for the leaves—you need three leaves for each rose, which you can cut from green crepe paper in one step.

3 Take four or five petals at a time and place them together on top of each other. Place a pencil on its side at the rounded end of the petals. Roll up tightly around the pencil and then slide the pencil out.

4 When you have curled all the flower petals, prepare the three leaves in the same way.

Paper know-how

Crepe paper is available in a good selection of bright colors. It stretches readily in one direction but not quite so easily at right angles to this. When you are cutting your petals, try to make the best use of the stretchy direction of the material.

Paper know-how

Crepe paper and tissue are among the lightest and most delicate of papers, but the dye in some of the colored varieties may bleed badly, so be careful if using them near pale-color fabrics—particularly if the paper is likely to become wet.

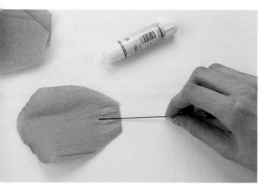

5 Place a dab of glue on the base of one of the petals. Take a short length of florists' wire and stick it onto the petal. Roll the petal around the wire.

6 Move around the wire, gluing the petals on one by one. Keep the inner petals wound tight and the outer petals more open, as on a real rose.

7 Take some florists' tape and start winding it around at the base of the rose, keeping the tape stretched as you go.

8 Start moving down the stem once you have covered the base of the flower, adding a leaf at intervals down the stem.

Snowflakes

I can remember making snowflakes as a child and the pleasure of opening out the folds to see what they looked like. Although they are made with just a humble piece of white paper and a few snips with the scissors, there is something very special about them. Grouped together in a window, they make a charming display, or use them to create a garland for the Christmas tree. This is a really easy project so everyone can get involved—put on some Christmas music and get the kids snipping!

you will need:

Sheets of white letter size (A4) paper

Scissors

Snowflake template on page 173

Tracing paper

Pencil

Glue stick

Thread (optional)

1 Fold up the left bottom corner of the paper to line up with the right edge. Cut off the spare rectangle of paper. You can use this to make small squares for tiny snowflakes. Make several different size squares to vary the snowflakes.

2 Fold the triangle in half. Then fold it in half again.

3 Use the tracing paper to transfer the snowflake design onto the folded paper triangle. Cut out the marked shapes. Instead of using the template, you could just snip away to make every snowflake different.

4 Open out the folded paper to reveal your snowflake.

5 To make a snowflake garland, simply place a dab of glue at the side edge of a snowflake and join it on to the next one. Carry on until you have the desired length. Alternatively, tie several snowflakes together with thread and hang.

Favor gift bags

Whether it is a children's party, birthday, or wedding, it is popular to give little gifts to your guests. I have used translucent paper for these pretty pouches; when made with a delicate scalloped edge and in pale pastel colors, they make a delightful gift bag for candy or sweets and little presents.

you will need:

Sheet of translucent patterned letter size (A4) paper

Pencil

Ruler

Scalpel or craft knife

Scissors with pointed tips

Double-sided adhesive tape

Small candies or gift to fill

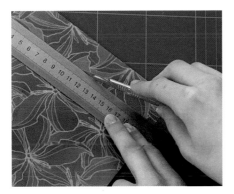

1 Measure and cut out an oblong of the paper measuring 5 x 6¾in. (12.5 x 17cm).

2 Cut a thin strip of double-sided adhesive tape approx. ¼in. (6mm) wide and 5in. (12.5cm) in length and place this along one of the 5in. (12.5cm) edges.

3 Remove the backing from the tape. Line up the two opposite edges and stick together, but don't flatten the curved pouch shape.

Sweet gifts

When using these little pouches to hold bonbons or other unwrapped candies, use paper that is greaseproof, otherwise the oils in the candy may stain it. Alternatively, place the candy inside a small plastic bag first.

4 Place a piece of tape inside one side of the bottom edge. Remove the backing and stick the bottom edges together, pressing firmly.

Extra decoration

I have made these gift bags in patterned paper, but an alternative would be to use plain paper and add another form of decoration. Look through other projects in this book for possible ideas, such as a name tag, tassel, crepe paper flower, or paper butterfly.

5 Place a few candies, or a small gift wrapped in tissue paper, into the pouch. Flatten down the tube at the open end in the opposite direction to the closed end, so that the glued side seam is positioned in the middle. This makes the pyramid shape. Press flat at each side edge with your fingers and thumbs to mark where to place the tape.

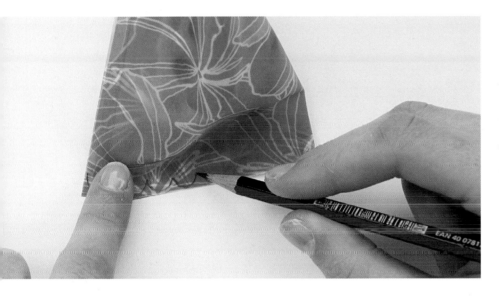

6 Place a strip of tape along one side on the inside of the top edge, lining up the ends to the creases at the side edges. Remove the tape backing and stick down the edges. With a pencil draw a line of scallops along both top and bottom seams.

7 Cut out the scallop edging along both edges, using a small pair of scissors with pointed tips.

Reindeer place names

Make your dinner party that extra bit special with these simple but stylish place cards. Your guests will love the little leaping reindeer; they will appreciate your creativity and want to take them home. Luckily the cards are easy to make so you can quickly rustle up some more! They would also make attractive festive gift tags or greetings cards.

you will need:

Reindeer template on page 173
Pencil
Tracing paper
Pieces of medium-thick white cardstock
Scalpel or craft knife
Cutting mat
Quilling paper
Quilling tool
Glue stick

1 Trace the template and transfer the reindeer shape onto some cardstock.

2 Cut out the outline of the shape using a scalpel or craft knife.

3 Take a length of quilling paper and place the end into the split at the top of the quilling tool. Start winding the paper around the tip of the tool, keeping it quite tight.

4 When you have finished winding, let the strip of paper go, so that it springs loose, and remove it gently from the tool. Make a few double-ended spirals by winding half the paper, and then removing it and attaching the other end to wind up in the opposite direction.

5 Put some glue over the antler part of the reindeer and position the quilled paper spirals to fill up the area. Vary the sizes of the coils to fit by opening them out or using them closed up.

Decoupage eggs

These decorative eggs will last a little longer than the chocolate variety that disappear very quickly on Easter morning! Arranged on a pretty plate, or with ribbons tied around them and hung from twigs of blossom, they make a charming spring display. I have used polystyrene eggs from a craft store for the base, but you could blow fresh eggs instead.

you will need:

Thin white paper

Scissors

Glue stick

Pieces of thin patterned paper

Polystyrene or blown fresh eggs

1 Cut strips of thin white paper ⅜in. (1cm) wide and approx. 3in. (7.5cm) in length.

2 Put glue on one side of each strip and, starting at the top, stick the strip down the length of the egg finishing at the bottom underneath. Repeat with the other strips. Overlap each strip slightly until you have covered the egg.

3 Cut out flowers, leaves, or other motifs from the patterned paper. I have used very pretty flocked paper from a craft store, but scraps of ordinary giftwrap paper would work just as well.

Tip

To blow a fresh egg, first wash the egg, then use a sharp needle to carefully prick a hole at least ⅛in. (3mm) in diameter at the top and bottom. Then blow through one hole to force the raw egg out through the other—you will find this easier if you break the yoke with the needle first.

4 Stick the flowers and leaves down carefully on the egg. Instead of covering the egg with white paper first, you could cut strips from the patterned paper and use these to cover the egg to make an all-over pattern.

Tools and materials

Essential tools

Scissors, small and large
Scalpel or craft knife
Cutting mat
Metal ruler
Hole punch, with different size heads
Hammer to use with the hole punch
Triangle (set square)
Pencils, hard 4 (2H) and softer 2 (HB)
Eraser
Something for scoring

Useful but not essential

Bone folder for making sharp creases
A soft brush to sweep away bits of
eraser

Paper and cardstock

Paper and cardstock come in different
weights, which is measured in grams
per square meter; the more grams,
the heavier and thicker the paper or
cardstock will be. For a project that
requires thick paper, use 120gsm;
if thin cardstock is specified, use
160gsm; and if you need thick
cardstock, use 200gsm. There is an
amazing array of different types of
paper that you can buy: beautifully
thick and textured handmade paper
from India; Japanese washi and
chiyogami papers in gorgeous
colors and patterns; fine, marbled
paper from Italy. Translucent, lacy,
flocked, sparkly—the choice is vast and
design combinations are endless.
Experiment with different types of
paper to change the look of projects,
be creative and consider all types.
I love to make something new out of
the old and I have a huge selection of
paper that I have collected over the
years: old labels with interesting
typography; maps; posters; comic
books; music sheets; candy wrappers.
Look out for old books that are falling
apart in flea markets—the aged cream
paper and elegant lettering will add
vintage charm to your designs.

Adhesives

I use different types of glue for different
projects and I also use different
adhesive tapes. With glue sticks, try to
find one with clear glue because this
type seems never to clog up. Wood
(PVA) glue is white when it goes on
but dries clear and is a very good
adhesive for large areas, such as the
steamboat project on page 44. Use a
brush or a small piece of cardstock to
apply it. Strong, quick-drying glue is
clear and usually comes in a tube. You
will need several types of adhesive
tape, for instance: masking tape,
double-sided tape, and clear tape.

Useful tips

These tips are useful techniques that
will either save you time or help to give
your projects a more professional look.

Enlarging templates

Some of the templates on pages 159–
173 will need to be enlarged and the
easiest way is on a photocopier—the
percentage enlargement you will need
is given. A few projects may not fit on
a tabloid size (A3) page. For these the
templates will have to be enlarged in
sections and joined together with tape.

Tracing

For many projects you need to transfer
the template onto paper or cardstock,
using tracing paper. Place a sheet of
tracing paper over the template and
secure with some masking tape. Trace
the lines with a hard 4 (2H) pencil, then
turn the tracing paper over and go
over the lines again on the reverse with
a softer pencil, such as a 2 (HB). Now
turn the tracing paper over again and
place it in position on your chosen
paper or cardstock. Go over all the
lines carefully with the 4 (2H) pencil,
and then remove the tracing paper.
This will give you a nice, clear outline.

Cutting

I use a scalpel or craft knife for nearly
all my projects. Make sure the blade is
sharp and that you always use a cutting
mat. When you need to make a straight
cut, use a metal ruler and keep the
blade in contact with the ruler at all
times. Cut toward you, keeping an
even pressure.

Scoring

It is important to score before making
any fold. If it helps, you can draw a
pencil line first to help you score in the
right place. Place a metal ruler along
the line and then score down the line,
using the back, blunt edge of a craft
knife or the blunt side of a cutlery knife.
Make sure you keep the side of the
blade in contact with the ruler.

Folding

Line up your edges carefully. Fold away
from you, creasing down with the
palm of your hand. Use a bone folder
if you want an extra sharp crease.

Templates

Framed bird paper cut (page 8)

Bird:
ENLARGE TO 250%

Foliage:
ENLARGE TO 250%

Wreath (page 12)

Leaf:
ENLARGE TO 125%

Lollipop flowers (page 14)

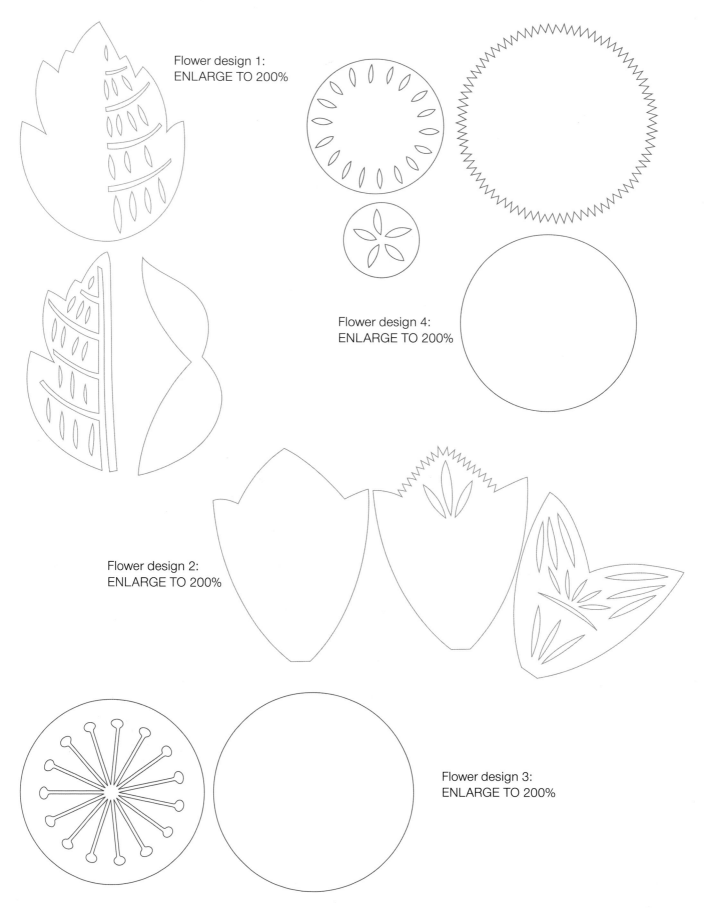

Flower design 1:
ENLARGE TO 200%

Flower design 4:
ENLARGE TO 200%

Flower design 2:
ENLARGE TO 200%

Flower design 3:
ENLARGE TO 200%

Sunflower (page 16)

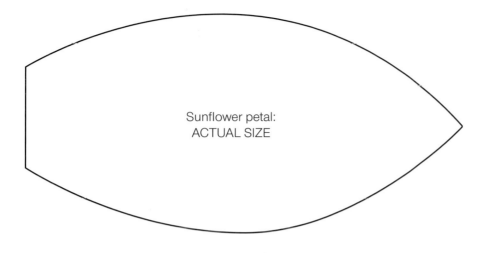

Sunflower petal:
ACTUAL SIZE

Hanging cutout birds (page 20)

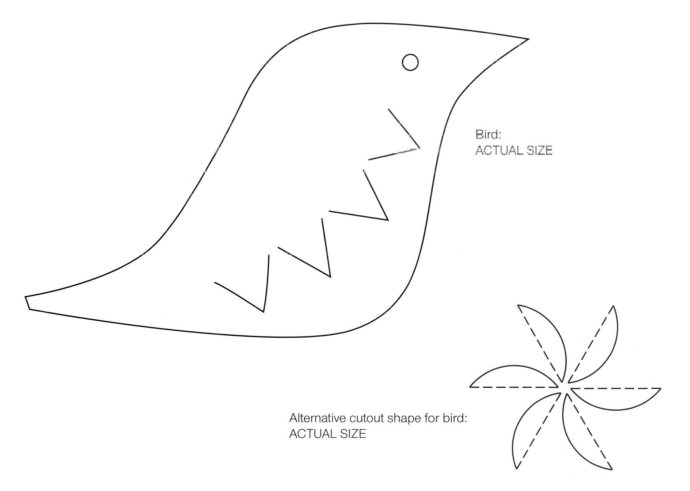

Bird:
ACTUAL SIZE

Alternative cutout shape for bird:
ACTUAL SIZE

Paper cut woodland scene (page 22)

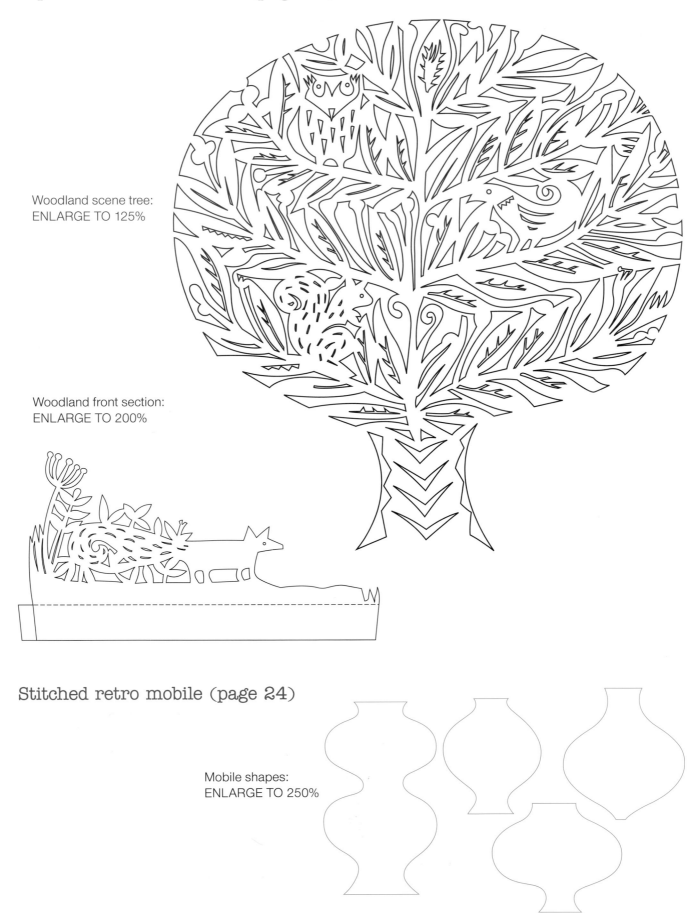

Woodland scene tree:
ENLARGE TO 125%

Woodland front section:
ENLARGE TO 200%

Stitched retro mobile (page 24)

Mobile shapes:
ENLARGE TO 250%

Paper chandelier (page 28)

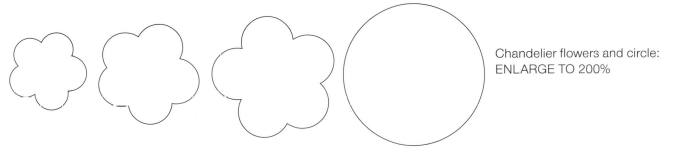

Chandelier flowers and circle:
ENLARGE TO 200%

Tealight houses (page 32)

Houses:
ENLARGE TO 400%

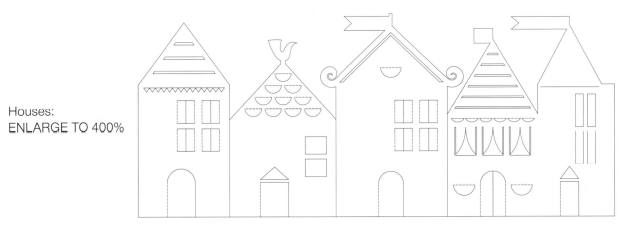

Love tealight lanterns (page 34)

Love lettering:
ENLARGE TO 200%

Bird boxes (page 38)

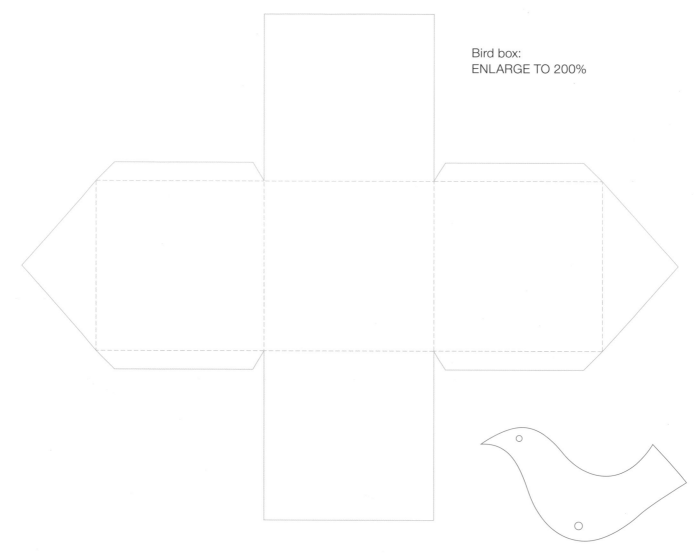

Bird box:
ENLARGE TO 200%

Bird box bird:
ENLARGE TO 200%

Curly tailed birds and nest (page 42)

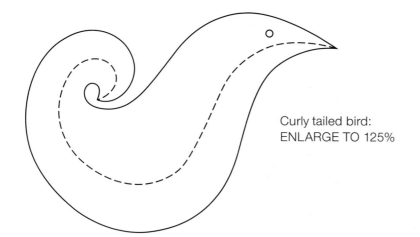

Curly tailed bird:
ENLARGE TO 125%

Steamboat (page 44)

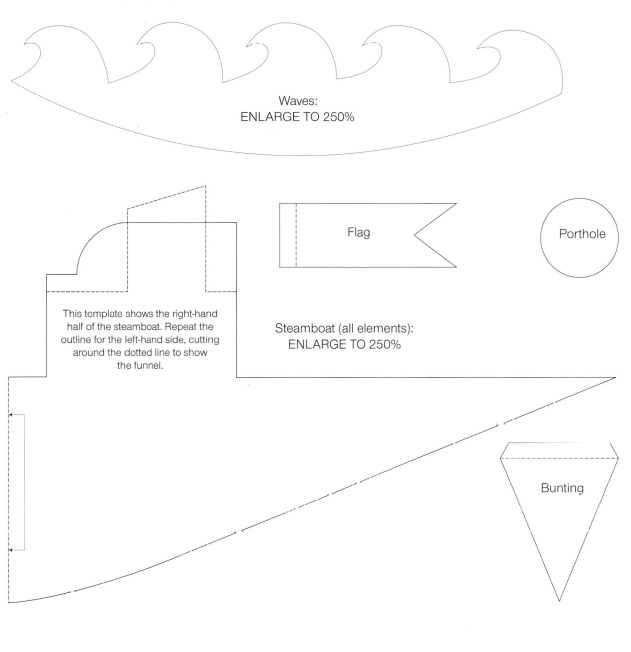

Waves:
ENLARGE TO 250%

Flag

Porthole

This template shows the right-hand half of the steamboat. Repeat the outline for the left-hand side, cutting around the dotted line to show the funnel.

Steamboat (all elements):
ENLARGE TO 250%

Bunting

Butterfly room divider (page 46)

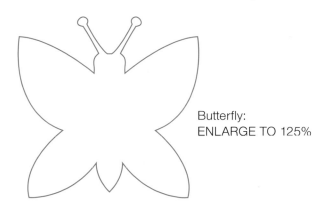

Butterfly:
ENLARGE TO 125%

Sausage dog (page 48)

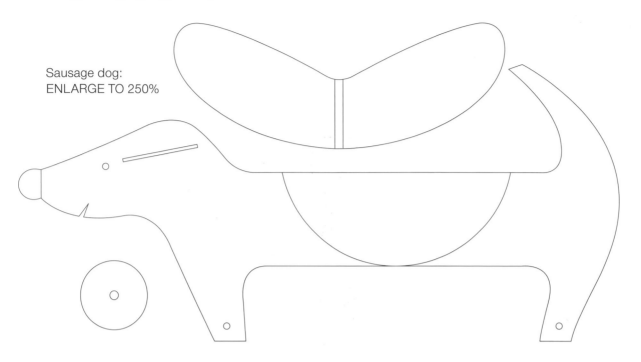

Sausage dog:
ENLARGE TO 250%

Swinging monkeys mobile (page 52)

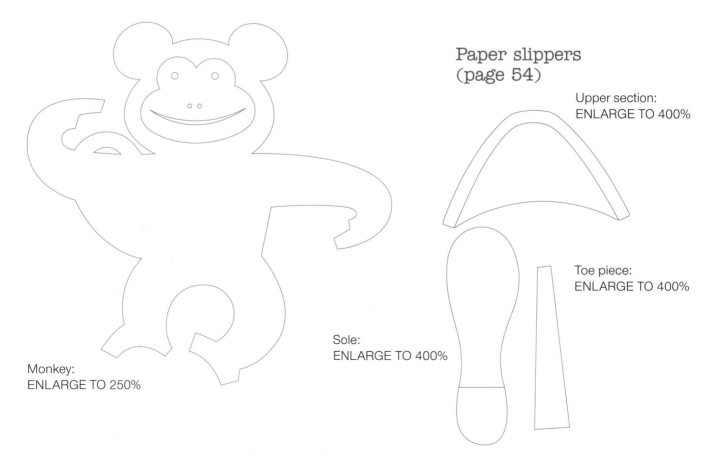

Paper slippers (page 54)

Upper section:
ENLARGE TO 400%

Toe piece:
ENLARGE TO 400%

Sole:
ENLARGE TO 400%

Monkey:
ENLARGE TO 250%

Clothespin dolls (page 60)

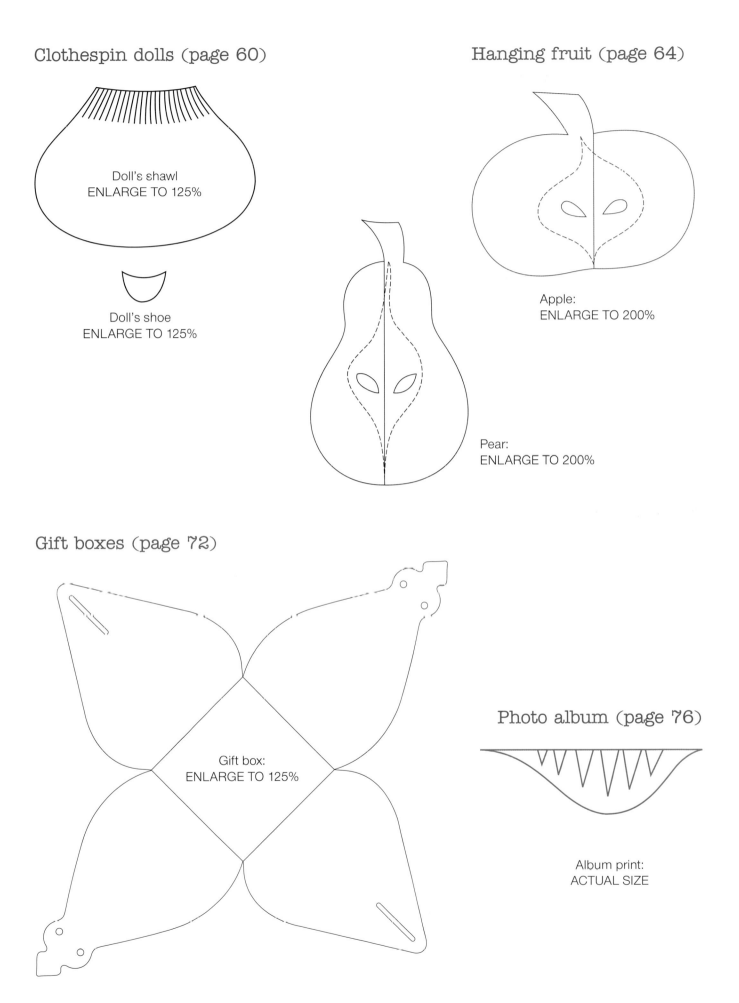

Doll's shawl
ENLARGE TO 125%

Doll's shoe
ENLARGE TO 125%

Hanging fruit (page 64)

Apple:
ENLARGE TO 200%

Pear:
ENLARGE TO 200%

Gift boxes (page 72)

Gift box:
ENLARGE TO 125%

Photo album (page 76)

Album print:
ACTUAL SIZE

Handprinted wrap and tags (page 84)

Wrap and tag print:
ACTUAL SIZE

Paper beads (page 90)

Experiment with different widths and
lengths to make beads of varying
shapes and sizes.

Bead:
ENLARGE TO 200%

Dragonfly clothespins (page 94)

Dragonfly:
ENLARGE TO 125%

Silver leaf fish (page 96)

Russian doll card (page 104)

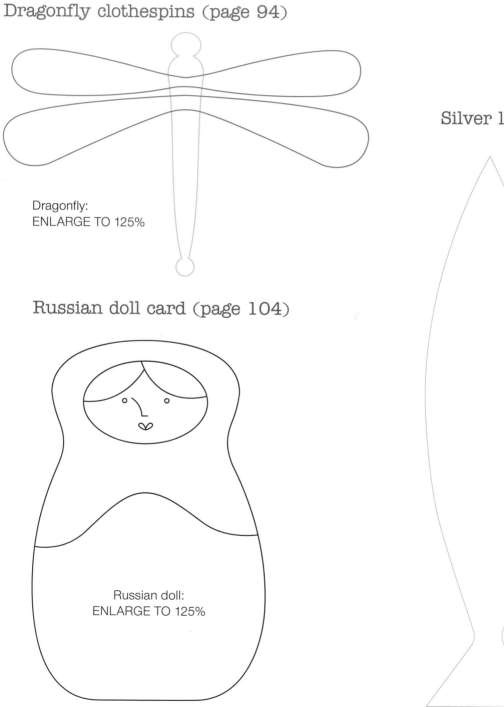

Russian doll:
ENLARGE TO 125%

Fish:
ENLARGE TO 400%

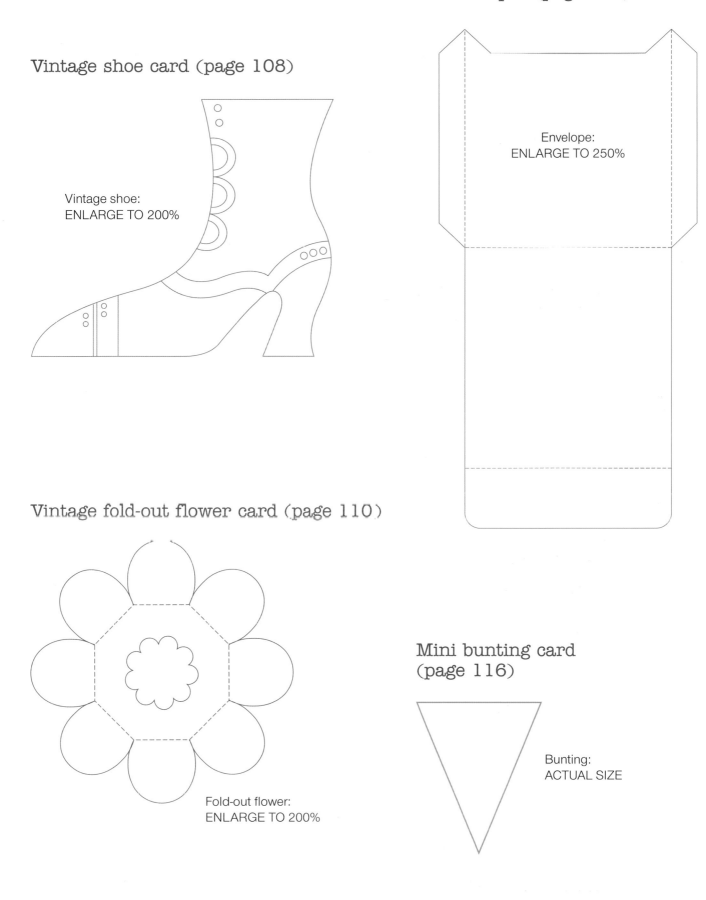

Vintage shoe card (page 108)

Vintage shoe:
ENLARGE TO 200%

Envelopes (page 114)

Envelope:
ENLARGE TO 250%

Vintage fold-out flower card (page 110)

Fold-out flower:
ENLARGE TO 200%

Mini bunting card
(page 116)

Bunting:
ACTUAL SIZE

Retro owl card
(page 118)

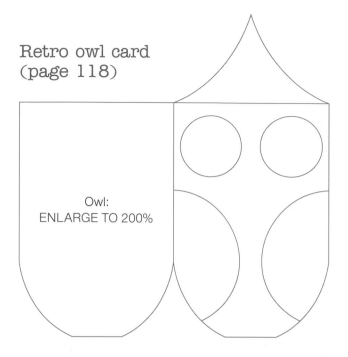

Owl:
ENLARGE TO 200%

Seahorse wrap and tags
(page 120)

Birdcage card (page 122)

Birdcage and bird:
ENLARGE TO 125%

Seahorse and wave:
ENLARGE TO 125%

Button nest card (page 126)

Robin and nest:
ENLARGE TO 125%

Filigree flower gift tag and card (page 130)

Filigree card and
tag pattern:
ACTUAL SIZE

Vintage floral cakestand (page 136)

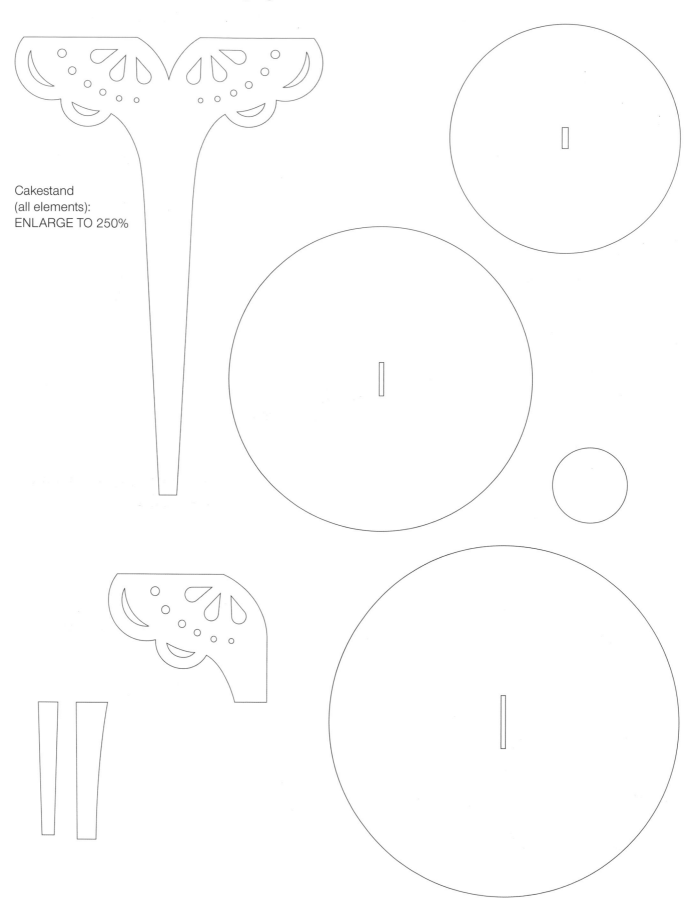

Cakestand
(all elements):
ENLARGE TO 250%

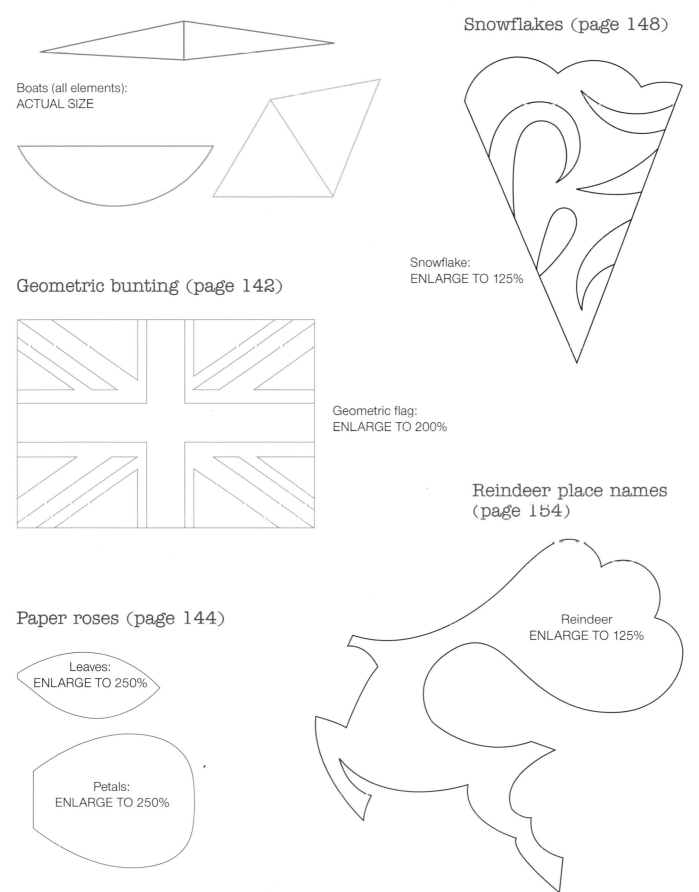

Cupcake toppers (page 140)

Boats (all elements):
ACTUAL SIZE

Geometric bunting (page 142)

Geometric flag:
ENLARGE TO 200%

Paper roses (page 144)

Leaves:
ENLARGE TO 250%

Petals:
ENLARGE TO 250%

Snowflakes (page 148)

Snowflake:
ENLARGE TO 125%

Reindeer place names (page 154)

Reindeer
ENLARGE TO 125%

Suppliers

US STOCKISTS

A.C. Moore
Stores nationwide
1-888-226-6673
www.acmoore.com

Art Supplies Online
Online store
1-800-967-7367
www.artsuppliesonline.com

Crafts, etc.
Online store
1-800-888-0321
www.craftsetc.com

Craft Site Directory
Useful online resource
www.craftsdirectory.com

Hobby Lobby
Stores nationwide
www.hobbylobby.com

Jo-Ann Fabric and Craft Store
Stores nationwide
1-888-739-4120
www.joann.com

Kate's Paperie
Stores across New York
1-800-809-9880
www.katespaperie.com

Michaels
Stores nationwide
1-800-642-4235
www.michaels.com

Paper Source
Stores nationwide
www.paper-source.com

UK STOCKISTS

Cass Art
Stores across London
020 7354 2999
www.cassart.co.uk

Craft Creations
Online store
01992 781900
www.craftcreations.com

Crafty Devils
Online store
01271 326777
www.craftydevilspapercraft.co.uk

Falkiners Fine Papers
London paper store
020 7831 1151
www.falkiners.com

Hobbycraft
Stores nationwide
01202 596100
www.hobbycraft.co.uk

Paperchase
Stores nationwide
www.paperchase.co.uk

The Papercraft Company
Online store
07812 575510
www.thepapercraftcompany.co.uk

Papercraft 4 You
Online store
02392 318097
www.papercraft4you.co.uk

Total Papercraft
Online store
01702 535696
www.totalpapercraft.co.uk

Index

Note: **Bold** page numbers refer to templates

Acknowledgments

I would like to thank all at CICO for giving me the opportunity to do what I enjoy most, and that is making things! A special thanks to Cindy, Pete, and Sally. Thanks to the designer, Jacqui Caulton, who has created such a stylish look. Thanks to Claire Richardson for her stunning photography and Ellie for all her help. Thanks to Martin Norris for his patience in producing such clear step photography and for having a great taste in music! Thanks also to Florence and Henrietta, two great hand models. Thank you Luka Seddon for the photo of Henrietta on the notebook project—a great photographer in the making! Thanks to Virginia at www.roddyandginger.co.uk for letting me use the lovely sun print in the magnet project and charming bird print in the retro mobile project. As always thank you to my family Ian, Milly, Florence, Henrietta, and Harvey for all their support. Finally, thank you to Ma Peggy and Pa, who gave me a craft book and a pile of paper at the age of eight and started the whole thing off!